REBUILD YOUR TEMPLE
GOD'S WAY®

FAITH AND HEALTH DEVOTIONAL
BIBLE STUDY WORKBOOK

*A COMPANION BIBLE STUDY GUIDE TO THE
30-DAY FAITH AND HEALTH DEVOTIONAL*

STEPHANIE L. FRANKLIN-SUBER

Dedication

To my faithful and steadfast husband, **Berchard V. Suber**, and to my son, **Michael Franklin Suber**—thank you for your resolute and unswerving love, prayers, and devotion throughout my nearly twenty-year journey to reclaim and maintain a life of health and wholeness.

Through cancer, chronic illness, and cardiac arrest, you walked beside me with perseverance, resilience, and courage. You are my beacons of hope and inspiration—daily reminders that love endures all things and that the mercy, compassion, and grace of our triune God truly sustain.

To **Reverend Anna Grant-Borden** and the members of **Mount Airy Presbyterian Church**, past, present, and future—may you be blessed for your faithful prayers, support, and partnership in ministry.

To every woman on the journey to health and wholeness—may the *Rebuild Your Temple, God's Way®* *Faith and Health Devotional* and this companion *Faith and Health Devotional Bible Study Workbook* become a sacred space of reverence, reflection, and revelation as you walk on this 30-day journey with the God who makes all things new.

May you discover the beauty of *Rebuilding Your Temple, God's Way®*. With utmost gratitude to my **Heavenly Father**, my Creator, to my **Lord and Savior**, **Jesus Christ**, and to the **Holy Spirit**, whose power restores, renews and aligns us—body, soul, and spirit.

May You be glorified.

Blessed by the support of Cathy Morenzie, Preston Squire, and Jennifer Eastmond, and by the gifted work of Alec Gerhart and Rachel Aponte.

Foreword

Do you not know that your body is a temple of the Holy Spirit who is within you, whom you have from God, and that you are not your own? You were bought with a price [you were actually purchased with the precious blood of Jesus and made His own]. So then, honor and glorify God with your body.
(1 Corinthians 6:19–20 AMP)

Our bodies are sacred edifices, masterfully created by God for His glory and for worship. In Psalm 19:1, King David declares, *"The heavens declare the glory of God; the skies proclaim the work of his hands."* Just as the heavens reflect the majesty of God, so do we — His beloved creation. We are the workmanship of His hands, *"fearfully and wonderfully made."*

Yet as we journey through life, the demands placed on our bodies — some self-imposed and others thrust upon us by circumstances, people, or illness — can leave us depleted, wounded, or disconnected from the God who created us. In these moments of weariness and brokenness, we stand in need of **restoration**, **renewal**, and **realignment** with our Creator.

In this beautifully architected and God-inspired devotional collection, Stephanie Franklin-Suber gently but powerfully guides you through a sacred journey to restore your body, renew your soul, and realign your spirit.

Stephanie has walked this very path — from brokenness into wholeness through the transformative power of God's Word. God miraculously healed and delivered her from cancer, from years of chronic illness, and most recently from cardiac arrest. In each chapter of her testimony, God revealed to her the sacredness of her temple and showed her that, through faith in Jesus Christ, through Scripture, and by the work of the Holy Spirit, her temple could be rebuilt — God's way. Today, God has called Stephanie to help others rebuild their temples: body, soul, and spirit.

It is with joy and deep gratitude that I introduce you to this ***Rebuild Your Temple, God's Way®*** ***Signature Faith and Health Collection***, which includes the three-book *10-Day Devotional Series* (*Restore Your Body*, *Renew Your Soul*, and *Realign Your Spirit*) and the two-book *30-Day Devotional Series* (the *30-Day Devotional* and the companion *Bible Study Workbook*).

As you embark on this sacred journey, do so with **anticipation** and **expectation**. Allow the Word of God to minister to your soul through Scripture and Reflection. Worship God with your body through the daily Temple Practice. Receive God's healing and restoration by engaging the Health Coaching Tips. And experience spiritual alignment as your spirit connects with the Spirit of God through prayer and journaling in the *Rebuild Your Temple, God's Way®* Journal.

It is my honor and delight to invite you to experience this transformational journey.
Come, and Rebuild Your Temple, God's Way®.

Yours in Christ,
Rev. Anna L. Grant-Borden
Senior Pastor, Mt. Airy Presbyterian Church
Philadelphia, Pennsylvania

Table of Contents

Daily Workbook Pages
Each day includes Word Study, Deeper Reflection, Faith in Action, Wellness Wisdom, Prayer and Praise, Revelation, and Declaration.

Author's Introduction

This *Rebuild Your Temple, God's Way® Faith and Health Bible Study Workbook* was created to accompany the *Rebuild Your Temple, God's Way® Faith and Health 30-Day Devotional* and the *Rebuild Your Temple, God's Way® Journal* to guide you into a deeper, more personal encounter with the triune nature of God.

Your body is one of God's greatest gifts—a sacred Triune Human Temple™ (Body–Soul–Spirit) where His Holy Spirit dwells. When God gave King David the design for the Holy Temple in Jerusalem, it reflected His triune nature: Father, Son, and Holy Spirit. The Temple had three parts—the *Outer Court*, the *Inner Court*, and the *Holiest of Holies*—each representing a deeper place of worship and intimacy with Him.

You, too, were created in God's triune image as a Triune Human Temple™ (Body–Soul–Spirit). The **body** personifies the *Outer Court*, where visible acts of stewardship and worship take place. The **soul**—your mind, will, and emotions—mirrors the *Inner Court*, where thoughts and desires are consecrated to Him. And your **spirit** embodies the *Holiest of Holies*, the inner sanctuary of communion with God.

The Triune Temple Journey™ structure of this *Bible Study Workbook* and the *30-Day Devotional* is modeled on the divine design of the Temple and the triune nature of God. It unites three progressively deeper journeys into your Triune Human Temple™ (Body–Soul–Spirit) into one 30-day rhythm:

- **Part I** – *Restore Your Body* (Days 1–10):
  Rebuild your *Outer Court* through nourishment, movement, and rest, honoring God the Father, by honoring your body.

- **Part II** – *Renew Your Soul* (Days 11–20):
  Enter your *Inner Court*, where God the Son, heals your emotional wounds and renews your mind with His peace.

- **Part III** – *Realign Your Spirit* (Days 21–30):
  Dwell in your *Holiest of Holies*, where God the Holy Spirit restores communion, brings your life into harmony with our triune God, and leads you into your God-given purpose.

These pages were born from my own story of *Rebuilding My Temple, God's Way®*—through cancer, chronic illness, and miraculous cardiac arrest—where God, in three persons, met me again and again with healing, hope, and restoration. The same God who restored me will meet you wherever you are in your faith and health journey and restore you too.

This is a sacred journey of rebuilding your temple—from the *Outer Court* to the *Inner Court* to the

Holiest of Holies for transformation from the outside in and the inside out.

As you move through each part—**Restore, Renew, and Realign**—you will rediscover what it means to live as the dwelling place of God: whole, healthy, and holy.

May the *Devotional,* this *Bible Study Workbook* and the *Journal* become your daily altar—a place of worship, wellness, and wonder—as you *Rebuild Your Temple, God's Way*®.

How to Use This Workbook

Teach me Your way, Lord, that I may rely on Your faithfulness;
give me an undivided heart, that I may fear Your name.
(Psalm 86:11 NIV)

This *Bible Study Workbook* was created to be used **side by side** with the *Rebuild Your Temple, God's Way® Faith and Health 30-Day Devotional.*

Each day in this *Bible Study Workbook* corresponds directly with a day in the *Devotional*—same title, Scripture, and theme—so that you can move from *inspiration* in this *Devotional* to *transformation* in this *Bible Study Workbook* through deeper study, reflection, and application.

You are encouraged to use the *Rebuild Your Temple, God's Way® Journal* or your own personal journal for more space to capture your prayers, insights, and breakthroughs in the *Devotional* and this *Bible Study Workbook.*

Each Daily Workbook Page includes seven Bible study elements: Word Study, Deeper Reflection, Faith in Action, Wellness Wisdom, Prayer and Praise, Revelation and Declaration.

Word Study: Explore the Daily Devotional Scripture, context, key words, and reflect on discovery questions.

Deeper Reflection: Engage in body, soul and spirit restoration, renewal and realignment work through deeper guided reflection and self-examination that fits the theme of the Daily Devotional.

Faith in Action: Apply what you have learned with the Devotional Temple Practice and what you have learned through one simple act of obedience.

Wellness Wisdom: Connect the Devotional Health Coaching Tip to biblical principles to promote holistic health in daily living.

Prayer and Praise: Pray the Daily Devotional Prayer, personalize it in your own words and comment on what resonates with you.

Revelation: Journal your thoughts, emotions, and spiritual insights.

Declaration: Speak life and truth over your day with the Devotional Affirmation and your personal faith-filled declaration for the day.

Suggested Daily Rhythm

1. **Begin with Prayer**
   Invite God in His three persons to speak as you open your *Devotional* and Bible.

2. **Read the Daily Devotional**
   Let the message settle in your heart before moving into this *Bible Study Workbook.*

3. **Reflect in the Daily Workbook Page**
   Complete each of the seven sections at your own pace—there is no rush. Use this time to

listen, write, and respond to what God is revealing.

4. **Record in Your Journal**

   If you need more space, use your *Rebuild Your Temple, God's Way® Journal* or your own personal Journal to capture prayers, insights, and revelations.

5. **Pray and Declare**

   Close your time by thanking God and speaking your Daily Declaration aloud.

Helpful Tips

- **Set a consistent time** each day for your *Devotional* and *Bible Study Workbook* study—morning quiet time or evening reflection.

- **Keep your Bible, Devotional, Bible Study Workbook, and Journal together** in one sacred space.

- **Mark your growth** by noting answered prayers or physical, emotional, or spiritual changes.

- **Track your progress** by using the **Faith and Health Habit Tracker** in the *Workbook* after this 30-day journey to continue your transformation.

- **Extend grace** to yourself—this journey is about progress, not perfection.

As you move from ***Restore*** to ***Renew*** to ***Realign***, remember that every healthy habit, every step of faith, every act of reflection, every prayer, and every declaration is rebuilding the dwelling place of the triune God within you—body, soul, and spirit.

May your body be strengthened by our Creator, may your soul be calmed by our Savior, and may your spirit be brought into harmony with the Holy Spirit.

May you enjoy and embrace this journey to *Rebuild Your Temple, God's Way®*.

Your 30-Day Triune Temple Journey™ At A Glance

Part	**Restore Your Body**	**Renew Your Soul**	**Realign Your Spirit**
Temple Sanctuary	Outer Court	Inner Court	Holiest of Holies
Triune Divine Person	God the Father	God the Son	God the Holy Spirit
Triune Human Temple™	Body	Soul	Spirit
Spiritual Focus	Worship through action	Worship through surrender	Worship through communion
Result	Strengthened stewardship and gratitude	Inner healing and renewed peace	Alignment and divine purpose

As you move through this Triune Temple Journey™, you will experience the beauty of transformation from the outside in and the inside out—restored in body, renewed in soul, and realigned in spirit.

May every page lead you deeper into the presence of the One who created you, redeemed you, and now dwells within you.

Understanding Your Triune Temple Journey™

A Visual Guide to God's Design of Your Triune Human Temple™ (Body–Soul–Spirit)

The structure of the Holy Temple in Jerusalem reveals a sacred pattern woven throughout Scripture—a pattern that also reflects the divine design of your own life.

Just as the Temple was made of three distinct sanctuaries—the *Outer Court*, the *Inner Court,* and the *Holiest of Holies*—your Triune Human Temple™ (Body–Soul–Spirit) is created with three interconnected sanctuaries: **body**, **soul**, and **spirit**.

This 30-day Triune Temple Journey™ follows that same holy progression.

You begin in the *Outer Court*, learning to honor God the Father with your physical body.

You move into the *Inner Court*, where God the Son heals and restores your mind, will, and emotions.

Finally, you enter the *Holiest of Holies*, where God the Holy Spirit dwells within you, guiding you into communion, alignment, and purpose.

As you study this Triune Temple Journey™ Temple Diagram, you will see how each sanctuary of the Holy Temple reflects your own Triune Human Temple™ as you journey toward health and wholeness—restored, renewed, and realigned in the presence of the triune God.

Triune Temple Journey™
TEMPLE DIAGRAM

Outer Court ➜ *Holy Place* ➜ *Holiest of Holies*
(Body ➜ *Soul* ➜ *Spirit)*

OUTER COURT
(Courtyard of the Temple)

Temple Sacred Elements:
Bronze Altar (Sacrifice/Obedience)
Bronze Laver (Washing/Cleansing)

GOD THE FATHER

RESTORE YOUR BODY
(Days 1 – 10)

INNER COURT
(Holy Place of the Temple)

Temple Sacred Elements:
Golden Lampstand (Light)
Table of Showbread (Provision)
Golden Altar of Incense (Prayer)

GOD THE SON

RENEW YOUR SOUL
(Days 11 – 20)

HOLIEST OF HOLIES
(Most Holy Place of the Temple)

Temple Sacred Elements:
The Veil (Access)
The Mercy Seat (Fellowship)
The Ark of the Covenant (God's Glory and Holy Presence)

GOD THE HOLY SPIRIT

REALIGN YOUR SPIRIT
(Days 21 – 30)

Triune Temple Journey™
TEMPLE DIAGRAM LEGEND

Understanding the Outer Court, the Inner Court, and the Holiest of Holies

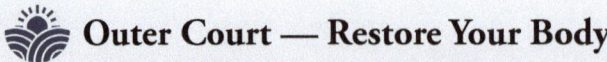 **Outer Court — Restore Your Body**

Temple Meaning: Where sacrifice and physical cleansing were performed.
Your Journey: *Days 1–10* focus on honoring God the Father with your physical body—through nourishment, hydration, movement, stillness, and rest.
Spiritual Symbol: Your **body** is the *Outer Court* of your Triune Human Temple™, a sacred place of stewardship and obedience to the Creator and Provider.

 Inner Court — Renew Your Soul

Temple Meaning: The Holy Place where priests tended the lampstand, table of showbread, and altar of incense.
Your Journey: *Days 11–20* invite God the Son to heal your heart, renew your mind, and align your emotions.
Spiritual Symbol: Your **soul**—mind, will, and emotions—is the *Inner Court* in your Triune Human Temple™ where the Prince Peace, the Living Word and Heavenly High Priest restores peace and truth.

 **Holiest of Holies — Realign Your Spirit**

Temple Meaning: God's dwelling place above the Ark of the Covenant.
Your Journey: *Days 21–30* guide you into intimate communion with the Holy Spirit—hearing His voice, walking in His power, and reflecting His glory.
Spiritual Symbol: Your **spirit** is the *Holiest of Holies* in your Triune Human Temple™ where the Spirit dwells, connects you to the triune God and leads you into purpose and transformation.

As you move through this Bible Study Workbook and the Faith and Health 30-Day Devotional, let the structure of God's Holy Temple remind you of the sacred design of your Triune Human Temple™, fearfully and wonderfully created in His image and indwelt by His presence.

Temple Illustration: Herod's Temple

Cut-Away View of the Outer Court, the Inner Court, and the Holiest of Holies

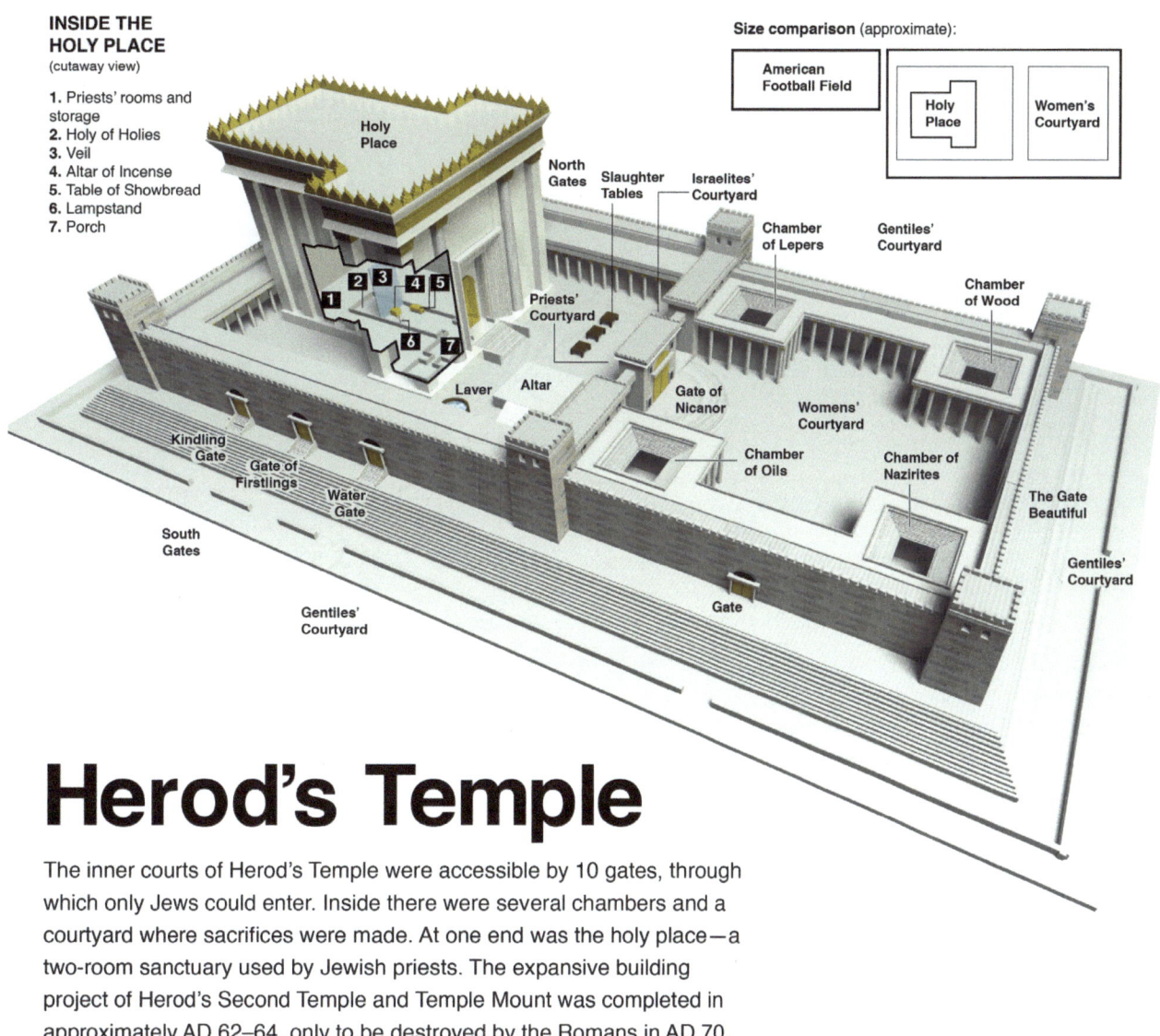

INSIDE THE HOLY PLACE
(cutaway view)

1. Priests' rooms and storage
2. Holy of Holies
3. Veil
4. Altar of Incense
5. Table of Showbread
6. Lampstand
7. Porch

Size comparison (approximate):

American Football Field

Holy Place

Women's Courtyard

Holy Place

North Gates

Slaughter Tables

Israelites' Courtyard

Chamber of Lepers

Gentiles' Courtyard

Chamber of Wood

Priests' Courtyard

Gate of Nicanor

Womens' Courtyard

Laver

Altar

Chamber of Oils

Chamber of Nazirites

The Gate Beautiful

Kindling Gate

Gate of Firstlings

Water Gate

South Gates

Gate

Gentiles' Courtyard

Gentiles' Courtyard

Herod's Temple

The inner courts of Herod's Temple were accessible by 10 gates, through which only Jews could enter. Inside there were several chambers and a courtyard where sacrifices were made. At one end was the holy place—a two-room sanctuary used by Jewish priests. The expansive building project of Herod's Second Temple and Temple Mount was completed in approximately AD 62–64, only to be destroyed by the Romans in AD 70.

PART I – RESTORE YOUR BODY

A 10-Day Journey with God the Father —
Worshiping the Creator by Stewarding Your Body

RESTORE

Restore Your Body. Renew Your Soul. Realign Your Spirit.™

Welcome to the Outer Court

This first part of your Triune Temple Journey™ begins in the *Outer Court*—the visible place of worship and obedience.

Here, you will walk with **God the Father**, your Creator and Sustainer, who lovingly designed your body as His dwelling place.

Just as the priests served in the *Outer Court* of the Temple through acts of offering and service, you, too, honor God through daily acts of stewardship of your health: nourishing your body, moving with gratitude, resting in trust, and breathing in His peace.

Each day in Part I will help you restore reverence for the sacred gift of your physical health while awakening deeper gratitude for God the Father's faithful provision.

In the *Outer Court*, you learn to worship God the Father through visible acts of obedience and care for your body. This is where transformation begins—presenting your physical temple as a living sacrifice of gratitude and discipline.

Your Focus in This Section

- **Honor God the Father** by caring for the temple He created.
- **Restore your body** through nourishment, hydration, movement, and rest.
- **Learn to listen** to what your body reveals about His presence and care.
- **Cultivate daily habits** that reflect stewardship, gratitude, and trust.

Prayer of Invitation

Heavenly Father,
Thank You for creating my body as Your temple and calling me to care for it with love and gratitude. As I begin this 10-day journey in the *Outer Court*, restore in me a reverent awareness of Your presence in every breath, meal, and moment of rest. Teach me to honor You through how I nourish, hydrate, move, and tend this body You have entrusted to me. May these next days become sacred steps of restoration—one act of worship at a time.
In Jesus' name, I pray, Amen.

Day Overview Table

Day	Title	Scripture (NIV)
1	Your Body Is a Temple	1 Corinthians 6:19–20
2	Nourish Your Temple	Genesis 1:29
3	Hydrate and Refresh	Genesis 2:6
4	Move with Grace	Psalm 139:14
5	Breathe and Release	Genesis 2:7
6	Be Still and Know Him	Psalm 46:10
7	Rest to Rebuild	Exodus 20:8–11
8	Listen to Your Body	1 Kings 19:5–6
9	Renew Your Strength	Isaiah 40:31
10	Celebrate Progress	Psalm 103:2–5

# DAY 1 – YOUR BODY IS A TEMPLE

Scripture

Do you not know that your bodies are temples of the Holy Spirit, who is in you, whom you have received from God? You are not your own; you were bought at a price. Therefore honor God with your bodies.
(1 Corinthians 6:19–20 NIV)

Scripture Focus:

God the Father purchased me with a price; my body belongs to Him and exists to honor His presence.

Theme Summary:

Wellness begins with reverence for the dwelling place of God the Father within me.

1 | Your Word Study

Context:

Corinth celebrated indulgence; Paul re-teaches honor for the body as sacred space.

Key Word:

Temple (naos) — the inner sanctuary where God the Father dwells.

Cross References:

- *1 Peter 1:18-19 (NIV) – For you know that it was not with perishable things such as silver or gold that you were redeemed … but with the precious blood of Christ, a lamb without blemish or defect.*
- *Romans 12:1 (NIV) – Therefore, I urge you, brothers and sisters, in view of God's mercy, to offer your bodies as a living sacrifice, holy and pleasing to God — this is your true and proper worship.*

Discovery Questions:

1. What changes when I see my body as the inner sanctuary of God the Father?

    _____

    _____

2. How does the price He paid to redeem me shape my daily choices?

_____

_____

3. What practice today will honor His presence in me?

_____

_____

2 | Your Deeper Reflection

Where have I treated this temple as common?

_____

_____

How can I show reverence through rest, nutrition, or boundaries this week?

_____

_____

How does viewing my physical body as God's temple reshape the way I think about my daily choices like rest, nourishment, or movement?

_____

_____

3 | Your Faith in Action

Apply the Devotional Temple Practice:
Choose one act of honor—prepare a wholesome meal, take a walk, or rest without guilt.

Record:
How did your body feel?

_____

_____

Next Step:
Repeat tomorrow as a daily offering.

4 | Your Wellness Wisdom

Revisit the Devotional Health Coaching Tip:
God the Creator designed sleep, nutrition, and movement as restorative systems. Stewarding them is obedience, not vanity.

5 | Your Prayer and Praise

Comment:
Which line in the Devotional Prayer most moved me?

_____

_____

My Prayer Response: _____

_____

_____

6 | Your Revelation

Journal Question:
What healthy boundaries will protect this dwelling place of God the Father in me?

_____

_____

_____

7 | Your Daily Declaration

Repeat the Devotional Affirmation:
I honor God by honoring my temple through every choice I make.

Today I will ... honor God the Father in my body through gratitude and stewardship.

 # DAY 2 – NOURISH YOUR TEMPLE

Scripture

So whether you eat or drink or whatever you do, do it all for the glory of God.
(1 Corinthians 10:31 NIV)

Scripture Focus:

Every bite and sip can reflect the glory of God the Father when offered in gratitude.

Theme Summary:

Eating becomes worship when my choices flow from thanksgiving and purpose.

1 |Your Word Study

Context:
Paul teaches believers to use freedom responsibly so God is honored in ordinary acts.

Key Word:
Glory (doxa) — the visible honor and weight of God's character.

Cross References:
- *Colossians 3:17 (NIV) – And whatever you do, whether in word or deed, do it all in the name of the Lord Jesus, giving thanks to God the Father through Him.*
- *Psalm 104:14-15 (NIV) – He makes grass grow for the cattle … bringing forth food from the earth: wine that gladdens human hearts, oil to make their faces shine, and bread that sustains their hearts.*

Discovery Questions:

1. How does gratitude for the provision of God the Father transform my table into an altar?

_____

_____

2. Which attitude—entitlement or thankfulness—guides my eating habits?

_____

_____

3. How can my food choices serve God the Father's purpose in my life?

_____

_____

2 | Your Deeper Reflection

When do I eat for comfort instead of strength?

_____

_____

How can I invite God the Father to restore peace to my relationship with food?

_____

_____

What small, consistent act of nourishment can I offer my body this week as an expression of gratitude to God the Father?

_____

_____

3 | Your Faith in Action

Apply the Devotional Temple Practice:
Pray before each meal today; eat slowly and savor each bite with thanksgiving.

Record:
Note how mindfulness and gratitude change your awareness.

_____

_____

Next Step:
Repeat tomorrow as a daily offering.

4 | Your Wellness Wisdom

Revisit the Devotional Health Coaching Tip:
Meals rich in fiber, protein, and color support steady energy. Eating with thankfulness activates the body's rest-and-digest response and reduces stress.

5 | Your Prayer and Praise

Comment:
How did today's Devotional Prayer reframe my dependence on the provision of God the Father?

_____

_____

My Prayer Response: _____

_____

_____

6 |Your Revelation

Journal Question:
What truth about His abundance is God the Father inviting me to believe at the table today?

_____

_____

_____

7 |Your Daily Declaration

Repeat the Devotional Affirmation:
I take every bite with gratitude to honor the God who sustains me.

Today I will ... eat mindfully to glorify God the Father who provides my daily bread.

 DAY 3 – HYDRATE AND REFRESH

Scripture

The Lord will guide you always; He will satisfy your needs in a sun-scorched land and will strengthen your frame. You will be like a well-watered garden, like a spring whose waters never fail.

(Isaiah 58:11 NIV)

Scripture Focus:

God the Father created my body to require the water He provides—every sip acknowledges His wisdom, design and care.

Theme Summary:

Hydrating my body is a daily act of obedience and gratitude to the Creator who sustains life.

1 | Your Word Study

Context:

Isaiah used powerful imagery to describe the nature of God's blessings and provision. Creation itself teaches dependence on God the Provider for a common need—water.

Key Word:

Water (hydor) — element of life and cleansing found throughout Scripture.

Cross References:

- *Genesis 2:10 (NIV) – A river watering the garden flowed from Eden; from there it was separated into four headwaters.*

- *Psalm 104:10-13 (NIV) – He makes springs pour water into the ravines ... They give water to all the beasts of the field ... The land is satisfied by the fruit of His work.*

Discovery Questions:

1. How does God's design for creation demonstrate His care for human needs?

_____

2. What simple practice will help me thank Him as I drink today?

_____

_____

3. How might neglecting hydration show disconnection from His provision?

_____

_____

2 |Your Deeper Reflection

When was the last time I truly thanked God the Father for clean water?

_____

_____

What does consistent hydration make possible for my health and service to Him?

_____

_____

When my body signals thirst, how might this cue be an invitation from God the Father to slow down and receive His care?

_____

3 |Your Faith in Action

Apply the Devotional Temple Practice:
Drink water upon waking, midday, and evening; each time pray, "Creator God, thank You for what You provide."

Record:
Energy and clarity changes throughout the day.

_____

_____

Next Step:
Pair hydration with a short Scripture reflection.

4 |Your Wellness Wisdom

Revisit the Devotional Health Coaching Tip:
Water comprises most of our blood and cells. Proper intake regulates temperature, flushes toxins, and improves focus. Dependence on water reminds us we are God's creatures, not self-sustainers.

5 |Your Prayer and Praise

Comment:
What phrase in today's Devotional Prayer best reflects God as Provider?

_____

_____

My Prayer Response: _____

_____

_____

6 |Your Revelation

Journal Question:
How does receiving water with gratitude train me to trust God the Father to provide my daily needs?

_____

_____

_____

7 |Your Daily Declaration

Repeat the Devotional Affirmation:
I am refreshed by the Living Water and strengthened to flourish.

Today I will … drink water with gratitude, honoring the God the Father who designed and sustains my body.

 DAY 4 – MOVE WITH GRACE

Scripture
For in Him we live and move and have our being.
(Acts 17:28 NIV)

Scripture Focus:
Every movement is a gift from God the Father. I live and move within His design and strength.

Theme Summary:
Movement is worship when I align my pace and posture with the Creator's grace.

1 | Your Word Study

Context:
Paul reveals to Greek philosophers that life and motion flow from the Creator, not from idols.

Key Word:
Move (kineo) — to set in motion, be carried along by divine energy.

Cross References:
- *Psalm 18:33 (NIV) – He makes my feet like the feet of a deer; He causes me to stand on the heights.*
- *Isaiah 40:31 (NIV) – But those who hope in the Lord will renew their strength. They will soar on wings like eagles; they will run and not grow weary, they will walk and not be faint.*

Discovery Questions:

1. How can movement become an expression of thanksgiving?

   _____

   _____

2. When do I feel most aware of the presence of God the Father in motion?

_____

_____

3. What fear or comparison must I release to move freely?

_____

_____

2 |Your Deeper Reflection

When has my body felt like a burden rather than a blessing?

_____

_____

What shift happens when I see movement as connection to the Creator?

_____

_____

How does intentional movement—walking, stretching, or gentle exercise—help me feel more connected to the sustaining presence of God the Father?

_____

_____

3 |Your Faith in Action

Apply the Devotional Temple Practice:
Dedicate today's movement to God the Father—stretch, walk, breathe deeply. Begin and end with thanks.

Record:
Mood or focus changes after moving.

_____

_____

Next Step:
Schedule one daily movement window this week.

4 |Your Wellness Wisdom

Revisit the Devotional Health Coaching Tip:
Gentle motion improves circulation, mobility, and energy. Rhythmic movement calms the nervous system and teaches the body the pace of grace.

5 |Your Prayer and Praise

Comment:
Which phrase in the Devotional Prayer invited me to move with joy?

_____

_____

My Prayer Response: _____

_____

_____

6| Your Revelation

Journal Question:
What word summarizes how God the Creator is inviting me to move this week (e.g., freely, gracefully, boldly)?

_____

_____

7 |Your Daily Declaration

Repeat the Devotional Affirmation:
I live, move, and have my being in God, and my motion is worship.

Today I will ... move with gratitude and grace, staying in step with the rhythm of God.

 DAY 5 – BREATHE AND RELEASE

Scripture

Then the Lord God formed a man from the dust of the ground and breathed into his nostrils the breath of life, and the man became a living being.

(Genesis 2:7 NIV)

Scripture Focus:

Every breath I take is the sustaining gift of God the Father, my Creator; releasing tension honors the One who gave me life.

Theme Summary:

The breath of God the Father gave me life; mindful breathing restores balance and peace to the body He formed from dust.

1 | Your Word Study

Context:

Humanity began with breath — the sacred exchange between Creator and creation. Every inhale is a reminder of divine intimacy and dependence.

Key Word:

Breathed (Hebrew naphach) — to blow or breathe life with intent, to infuse spirit into clay.

Cross References:

- *Job 33:4 (NIV) – The Spirit of God has made me; the breath of the Almighty gives me life.*
- *Psalm 150:6 (NIV) – Let everything that has breath praise the Lord. Praise the Lord.*

Discovery Questions:

1. How does remembering God the Father as the source of my every breath change how I move through the day?

_____

_____

2. What emotions or burdens do I need to release as I exhale?

_____

_____

3. How does my breathing reflect the rhythm of rest and trust in my Creator?

_____

_____

2 | Your Deeper Reflection

When was the last time I stopped to simply breathe in gratitude?

_____

_____

How does shallow breathing mirror the pace of my thoughts or anxieties?

_____

_____

What might change if I used my breath to slow down, pray, and listen to God the Father?

_____

_____

3 | Your Faith in Action

Apply the Devotional Temple Practice:
Pause three times today for **intentional breathing**:

- **Inhale:** "Lord, You give me life."

- **Exhale:** "I release what I cannot control."

Record:
Notice how your body and mind respond.

_____

_____

Next Step:
Add one minute of deep breathing to your morning and evening rhythm this week.

4 | Your Wellness Wisdom

Revisit the Devotional Health Coaching Tip:
Breath is foundational to every bodily function. Deep, diaphragmatic breathing increases oxygen flow, calms the nervous system, and supports circulation. God the Father designed breath to connect body, soul and spirit— exhale as worship, inhale as restoration.

5 | Your Prayer and Praise

Comment:
What part of the Devotional Prayer reminded me that life itself is a gift from my Creator?

_____

_____

My Prayer Response: _____

_____

_____

6 | Your Revelation

Journal Question:
What burden do I need to release to calm my nervous system and breathe freely in my body again?

_____

_____

_____

7 | Your Daily Declaration

Repeat the Devotional Affirmation:
I receive God's peace and release my burdens with each breath I take.

Today I will ... breathe deeply, remembering that every breath is the gift of life from my Creator.

 # DAY 6 – BE STILL AND KNOW HIM

Scripture

Be still, and know that I am God; I will be exalted among the nations, I will be exalted in the earth.
(Psalm 46:10 NIV)

Scripture Focus:

Stillness honors God the Father as Creator and Sustainer, inviting His peace to steady my body and renew my strength.

Theme Summary:

Quieting my body creates space to sense the presence of God the Father and restore balance within His perfect design.

1 | Your Word Study

Context:

Psalm 46 proclaims God's power in the midst of chaos. "Be still" is not passive—it is an act of surrender, resting the body and trusting the Father's sovereignty.

Key Word:

Still (Hebrew raphah) — to let go, relax, release grip; to cease striving.

Cross References:

- *Exodus 14:14 (NIV) – The Lord will fight for you; you need only to be still.*
- *Mark 4:39 (NIV) – He got up, rebuked the wind and said to the waves, "Quiet! Be still!" Then the wind died down and it was completely calm.*

Discovery Questions:

1. What does physical stillness reveal about my trust in God the Father?

_____

_____

2. Where am I striving to control what belongs in His hands?

_____

_____

3. How can I create a rhythm of stillness in my daily life?

_____

_____

2 | Your Deeper Reflection

When was the last time I truly rested without multitasking or guilt?

_____

_____

What happens in my body when I slow down—heartbeat, breathing, awareness?

_____

_____

How does stillness allow me to hear the whisper of God the Father more clearly?

_____

_____

3 | Your Faith in Action

Apply the Devotional Temple Practice:
Set aside five minutes today to be completely still—no phone, no computer, no TV, no noise. Focus on your breath and repeat:

- "You are God."
- "I am still."

Record:
How did your body respond to stillness?

_____

_____

Next Step:
Schedule a brief stillness break at least once each day this week.

4 | Your Wellness Wisdom

Revisit the Devotional Health Coaching Tip:
Stillness is essential to recovery. Quiet moments slow heart rate, reduce blood pressure, and balance stress hormones. God the Father designed relaxation to repair what striving breaks—be still, and let Him rebuild your body through stillness in His loving presence.

5 | Your Prayer and Praise

Comment:
What phrase in today's Devotional Prayer reminded me to be still and rest in the strength and protection of God the Father?

_____

_____

My Prayer Response: _____

_____

_____

6 | Your Revelation

Journal Question:
Where is God the Father inviting me to "cease striving" and let Him handle the outcome?

_____

_____

_____

7 | Your Daily Declaration

Repeat the Devotional Affirmation:
I find God's strength and peace in stillness.

Today I will ... choose stillness over striving, trusting that God the Father is in control.

 **DAY 7 – REST TO REBUILD**

Scripture

In vain you rise early and stay up late, toiling for food to eat—for He grants sleep to those He loves.
(Psalm 127:2 NIV)

Scripture Focus:

God the Father lovingly gives sleep; striving without rest is empty. Receiving sleep is an act of trust and obedience.

Theme Summary:

Rest is not wasted time but worship — alignment with the Creator's design that rebuilds the body He entrusted to me.

1 | Your Word Study

Context:

Psalm 127 (a Song of Ascents, of Solomon) contrasts anxious self-effort with God-dependent living. Work without God's blessing is "vain"; rest is His gracious gift.

Key Word:

Vain (Hebrew shav') — empty, futile, without lasting result.

Cross References:

- *Psalm 4:8 (NIV) – In peace I will lie down and sleep, for You alone, LORD, make me dwell in safety.*
- *Mark 6:31 (NIV) – Then, because so many people were coming and going that they did not even have a chance to eat, He said to them, "Come with Me by yourselves to a quiet place and get some rest."*

Discovery Questions:

1. Where am I tempted to trade sleep for "just a little more" work?

_____

_____

2. How does receiving the gift of sleep express faith in the Father's provision and protection?

_____

_____

3. What healthy boundary would move my nights from anxious toil to peaceful rest?

_____

_____

2 | Your Deeper Reflection

Do I treat sleep as holy stewardship or optional luxury?

_____

_____

What beliefs (fear of failure, perfectionism, people-pleasing) keep me up late or up too early?

_____

_____

What would it look like to let God the Father "grant sleep" to me tonight?

_____

_____

3 | Your Faith in Action

Apply the Devotional Temple Practice:
Create a simple **wind-down liturgy** tonight (no telephones, computer or TV screens 30–60 min before bed; light stretch; prayer of release).

Record:
How did your body respond?

_____

_____

Next Step:
Set a consistent bedtime this week as a covenant of trust.

4 | Your Wellness Wisdom

Revisit the Devotional Health Coaching Tip:
Consistent sleep (7–9 hours for most adults) supports hormone balance, immune function, memory consolidation, and appetite regulation. The Creator hard-wired repair of your body throughout the night; surrendering to sleep is partnering with His design.

5 | Your Prayer and Praise

Comment:
Which phrase in the Devotional Prayer helped me release control to God the Father at bedtime?

_____

_____

My Prayer Response: _____

_____

_____

6 | Your Revelation

Journal Question:
What one change to my evening routine will help me receive the Father's gift of sleep?

_____

_____

_____

7 | Your Daily Declaration

Repeat the Devotional Affirmation:
I receive God's gift of rest and awake restored.

Today I will ... honor God the Father by receiving His gift of sleep and letting my body rebuild.

🌅 DAY 8 – LISTEN TO YOUR BODY

Scripture

Then he lay down under the bush and fell asleep. All at once an angel touched him and said, "Get up and eat." He looked around, and there by his head was some bread baked over hot coals, and a jar of water. He ate and drank and then lay down again.

(1 Kings 19:5–6 NIV)

Scripture Focus:

Before restoring Elijah's spirit, God the Father restored his body. The Creator cares for physical needs as part of His healing and restorative work.

Theme Summary:

Listening to the body's signals is an act of humility and obedience, allowing God the Father to rebuild physical strength before deeper renewal begins.

1 | Your Word Study

Context:

Exhausted and afraid, Elijah fled into the wilderness after Mount Carmel. Instead of rebuke, God sent sleep, food, and water—meeting Elijah's physical needs before addressing his soul.

Key Word:

Touched (Hebrew naga) — to reach, strike gently, or make contact to bring change or awakening.

Cross References:

• *Psalm 103:13–14 (NIV) – As a father has compassion on his children, so the Lord has compassion on those who fear Him; for He knows how we are formed, He remembers that we are dust.*
• *Matthew 11:28–29 (NIV) – Come to Me, all you who are weary and burdened, and I will give you rest. Take My yoke upon you and learn from Me, for I am gentle and humble in heart, and you will find rest for your souls.*

Discovery Questions:

1. What does His care for Elijah's physical exhaustion teach me about His priorities?

_____

_____

2. How can I practice receiving the gift of physical rest as part of my obedience?

_____

_____

3. When my body signals fatigue, hunger, or tension, how might that be the Father's invitation to pause?

_____

_____

2 | Your Deeper Reflection

Do I often try to "push through" exhaustion instead of listening to my body's limits?

_____

_____

What patterns of overwork or neglect might be dulling my sensitivity to the voice of the Father?

_____

_____

Where is He inviting me to slow down and receive care without guilt?

_____

_____

3 | Your Faith in Action

Apply the Devotional Temple Practice:
Today, honor one message from your body—rest, eat, hydrate, or breathe deeply.

Record:
How did responding to that cue change your energy or peace?

_____

_____

Next Step:
Build a daily check-in: "Father, how can I care for the body You have entrusted to me?"

4 | Your Wellness Wisdom

Revisit the Devotional Health Coaching Tip:
Ignoring signals of fatigue or hunger weakens both body and focus. Listening restores balance. God the Father designed physiological rhythms—nourishment, hydration, sleep—to support His divine design and our divine assignment. Obedience includes self-compassion.

5 | Your Prayer and Praise

Comment:
What phrase from the Devotional Prayer revealed the compassion of God the Father for my physical limits?

_____

_____

My Prayer Response: _____

_____

_____

6 | Your Revelation

Journal Question:
Which physical rhythm—sleep, nourishment, or rest—is the Father calling me to honor more faithfully this week?

_____

_____

_____

7 | Your Daily Declaration

Repeat the Devotional Affirmation:
I am fearfully and wonderfully made; I listen to my body with grace.

Today I will ... honor my body's God-given limits, receiving His care with gratitude and humility.

 # DAY 9 – RENEW YOUR STRENGTH

Scripture

He gives strength to the weary and increases the power of the weak. Even youths grow tired and weary, and young men stumble and fall; but those who hope in the Lord will renew their strength. They will soar on wings like eagles; they will run and not grow weary, they will walk and not be faint.

(Isaiah 40:31 NIV)

Scripture Focus:

When my strength fades, God the Father restores it. Waiting on Him replenishes my body with His divine energy.

Theme Summary:

Restoration comes from God, the Father, not my effort alone. Physical endurance flows from dependence on the Creator who empowers me to persevere.

1 | Your Word Study

Context:

Isaiah contrasts human limitation with God the Father's inexhaustible strength. Those who depend on Him experience renewal that exceeds natural capacity.

Key Word:

Renew (Hebrew chalaph) — to exchange, refresh, or replace with something new.

Cross References:

- *Psalm 103:2–5 (NIV) – Praise the Lord, my soul, and forget not all His benefits—who forgives all your sins and heals all your diseases, who redeems your life from the pit and crowns you with love and compassion, who satisfies your desires with good things so that your youth is renewed like the eagle's.*

- *2 Corinthians 12:9–10 (NIV) – But He said to me, "My grace is sufficient for you, for My power is made perfect in weakness." Therefore I will boast all the more gladly about my weaknesses, so that Christ's power may rest on me... For when I am weak, then I am strong.*

Discovery Questions:

1. What does it mean to "exchange" my weakness for the strength of God the Father?

   _____

   _____

2. How has weariness affected my stewardship of the body the Creator gave me?

   _____

   _____

3. What new rhythm of rest, nutrition, or movement might create space for restoration?

   _____

   _____

2 | Your Deeper Reflection

Where have I been relying on my own strength instead of the sustaining power of God the Father?

_____

_____

What physical or emotional signs tell me I am "running on empty"?

_____

_____

How can I invite the Creator into my moments of exhaustion and recovery?

_____

_____

3 | Your Faith in Action

Apply the Devotional Temple Practice:
Take one restorative action today—stretching, walking, a nourishing meal, or an early bedtime—while meditating on Isaiah 40:31.

Record:
How did your energy or mindset shift afterward?

_____

_____

Next Step:
Establish one restoration habit to repeat this week as a form of worship.

4 | Your Wellness Wisdom

Revisit the Devotional Health Coaching Tip:
The body rebuilds through proper rest, nutrition, and gentle activity. Overexertion drains vitality, but recovery strengthens resilience. The Father invites us to trade striving for steady rhythms of physical restoration.

5 | Your Prayer and Praise

Comment:
What part of the Devotional Prayer reminded me that God the Father is the source of my strength?

_____

_____

My Prayer Response: _____

_____

_____

6 | Your Revelation

Journal Question:
In what area of life is the Father asking me to slow down and let Him restore me instead of pushing harder?

_____

_____

_____

7 | Your Daily Declaration

Repeat the Devotional Affirmation:
I wait on the Lord, and He renews my strength daily for His purpose.

Today I will ... lean on God's strength, not my own, and let Him renew my energy and endurance.

DAY 10 – CELEBRATE YOUR PROGRESS

Scripture
Being confident of this, that He who began a good work in you will carry it on to completion until the day of Christ Jesus.
(Philippians 1:6 NIV)

Scripture Focus:
Each step of progress is evidence of God the Father's continuing work in me; celebration is gratitude for His faithfulness.

Theme Summary:
Growth in honoring my body is not the pursuit of perfection but the pursuit of partnership with God the Father. Rejoicing in small victories strengthens my perseverance.

1 | Your Word Study

Context:
Paul writes to encourage believers to stay confident that God the Father will finish what He starts. Physical transformation is part of that sanctifying work when surrendered to Him.

Key Word:
Begun (Greek enarchomai) — to start something sacred or inspired; to commence a work of grace that will be completed by God Himself.

Cross References:
• *Psalm 126:3 (NIV) – The Lord has done great things for us, and we are filled with joy.*
• *1 Thessalonians 5:23–24 (NIV) – May God Himself, the God of peace, sanctify you through and through… The One who calls you is faithful, and He will do it.*

Discovery Questions:

1. What evidence of progress has God the Father already produced in my health and habits?

_____

2. Why is it important to pause and thank Him before striving for the next goal?

_____

_____

3. How does celebration build motivation for continued obedience?

_____

_____

2 | Your Deeper Reflection

How often do I measure success by visible change rather than daily faithfulness?

_____

_____

What small victories—better choices, consistency, or patience—deserve recognition today?

_____

_____

How can I celebrate progress in a way that gives glory to the Creator, not to myself?

_____

_____

3 | Your Faith in Action

Apply the Devotional Temple Practice:
Mark one tangible improvement from the past week (hydration, rest, movement, mindful eating).

Record:
How did obedience feel in that area?

_____

_____

Next Step:
Plan a simple, God-honoring celebration—worship music, gratitude journal entry, or testimony shared with a friend.

4 | Your Wellness Wisdom

Revisit the Devotional Health Coaching Tip:
Celebration reinforces positive neural pathways and joy. Gratitude lowers stress hormones and increases resilience. God the Father designed rejoicing to sustain momentum— "*The joy of the Lord is your strength*" (Nehemiah 8:10 NIV).

5 | Your Prayer and Praise

Comment:
Which line from the Devotional Prayer stirred gratitude for progress made?

_____

_____

My Prayer Response: _____

_____

_____

6 | Your Revelation

Journal Question:

What new awareness or discipline has God the Father developed in me through this ten-day body-stewardship journey?

_____

_____

_____

7 | Your Daily Declaration

Repeat the Devotional Affirmation:

I rejoice in every step God helps me take toward health and wholeness.

Today I will ... celebrate every sign of growth, giving thanks that God the Father is completing His good work in me.

My Temple Reflection – Restore Your Body

A Time of Gratitude, Stewardship, and Strength

I praise You because I am fearfully and wonderfully made;
Your works are wonderful, I know that full well.
(Psalm 139:14 NIV)

Leaving the Outer Court

You have completed the first ten days of your Triune Temple Journey™—restoring your body and learning to worship **God the Father** through daily acts of stewardship.

Pause here to give thanks for what has been strengthened, released, or renewed in your physical temple.

Each choice to rest, hydrate, nourish, and move with grace was an act of obedience and faith.

Your Temple Reflection marks your visible progress and your deeper surrender to the One who designed you in His image.

My Body Work – Reflection Prompts

1. My Progress

What new physical habits or routines have I begun that bring me closer to health and wholeness?

_____

_____

Where have I noticed increased energy, peace, or gratitude in caring for my body?

_____

_____

2. My Lessons

What have I learned about the faithfulness of God the Father through caring for my physical health?

_____

_____

Where is the Father still inviting me to deeper consistency or trust?

_____

_____

3. My Gratitude

What blessings have I experienced over these ten days?

_____

_____

How has my awareness of the presence of God the Father grown through the stewardship of my body? *(Use the space below or use the Rebuild Your Temple, God's Way® Journal to write your reflections.)*

_____

_____

My Prayer of Thanksgiving

Heavenly Father,
Thank You for restoring my strength and reminding me that my body is Your temple.
You have taught me to rest as worship, to nourish as obedience, and to move as praise.
Continue to guide me as I honor You with my physical health, my new habits, and my thankful heart.
Let every bite, breath and step become an offering of gratitude to You.
In Jesus' name, I pray, Amen.

My Gratitude Offering

List three ways God the Father has revealed His goodness through this first part of your Triune Temple Journey™:
(Use this space or use the Rebuild Your Temple, God's Way® Journal to record a short note of thanks or a favorite verse that strengthened you during Part I.)

1. _____

2. _____

3. _____

My Extended Reflection

Continue your reflection by recording your progress in your Rebuild Your Temple, God's Way® Journal. Use it to note new habits, gratitude, and answered prayers as you grow in daily stewardship of your body.

My Transition to the Inner Court

*As I leave the **Outer Court** of visible worship,*
*I enter the **Inner Court**—where God the Son renews my soul and restores my peace.*

PART II – RENEW YOUR SOUL

A 10-Day Journey with God the Son —
Healing and Renewing Your Mind, Will, and Emotions

RENEW

Restore Your Body. Renew Your Soul. Realign Your Spirit.™

Welcome to the Inner Court

You are now entering the *Inner Court*—the sacred space where your thoughts, emotions, and desires are consecrated to God.

Here, in the middle part of your Triune Temple Journey™, you meet **God the Son**, your Redeemer and Healer, who restores peace to troubled hearts and transforms the patterns of your mind through His truth and grace.

In this space, your soul—your mind, will, and emotions—becomes the altar of surrender.

You bring your worries, fears, and wounds to Him, and in exchange, He gives you rest, renewal, and hope.

The next ten days in Part II are about learning to trust the compassion of Christ Jesus to release what weighs heavy on your heart, and to receive His healing presence.

This is where the beauty of emotional health and mindset renewal begins — not by striving to fix yourself but by resting in His love.

Your Focus in This Section

- **Encounter God the Son** — who heals, restores, and renews your inner life.
- **Renew your mind** through Scripture and gratitude.
- **Release emotional burdens** by bringing them to Jesus in prayer.
- **Cultivate peace and joy** that come from surrendering to His truth.

Prayer of Invitation

Lord Jesus,
I welcome You into the *Inner Court* of my soul. You know the thoughts that trouble me, the emotions that weigh me down, and the mistakes and regrets that still ache. Today, I invite You to renew my mind with Your Word and heal my heart with the peace of Your presence. Teach me to lay down my burdens and to rest in Your grace. Help me see myself and others through the lens of Your love. As I walk through these ten days, may my heart grow softer, my mind clearer, and my inner life more peaceful. Thank You for the promise that in You, all things are made new.
In Your name, I pray, Amen.

Day Overview Table

Day	Title	Scripture (NIV)
11	Guard Your Heart	Proverbs 4:23
12	Renew Your Mind	Romans 12:2
13	Lay It Down	Matthew 11:28
14	Overcome Your Fear	Isaiah 41:10
15	Choose Peace	John 14:27
16	Rest in His Grace	Ephesians 2:8–9
17	Reframe the Storm	Mark 4:39
18	Heal Your Broken Heart	Psalm 147:3
19	Cultivate Joy	Psalm 16:11
20	Walk in Freedom	Galatians 5:1

 # DAY 11 – GUARD YOUR HEART

Scripture

Above all else, guard your heart, for everything you do flows from it.
(Proverbs 4:23 NIV)

Scripture Focus:

The heart is the wellspring of my emotions, motives, and choices. Protecting it means letting God the Son rule what enters, what is released and what remains.

Theme Summary:

Renewal of the soul begins with awareness and boundaries. When I guard my heart through Christ Jesus, His peace governs my inner life.

1 | Your Word Study

Context:

Proverbs 4 gathers Solomon's counsel to his son: wisdom must be protected like treasure. In Hebrew thought, the *heart* is the control center of mind, will, and emotions.

Key Word:

Guard (Hebrew nātsar) — to keep watch, preserve, maintain with care.

Cross References:

- *Philippians 4:6–7 (NIV) – Do not be anxious about anything, but in every situation, by prayer and petition, with thanksgiving, present your requests to God. And the peace of God, which transcends all understanding, will guard your hearts and your minds in Christ Jesus.*

- *John 14:27 (NIV) – Peace I leave with you; My peace I give you. I do not give to you as the world gives. Do not let your hearts be troubled and do not be afraid.*

Discovery Questions:

1. What thoughts or influences most easily disturb the peace of my heart?

_____

_____

2. How does prayer act as protection against emotional or mental overload?

_____

_____

3. What boundaries would keep my heart centered on the truth and peace of Christ Jesus?

_____

_____

2 | Your Deeper Reflection

Where do I allow stress, comparison, or offense to invade my peace?

_____

_____

How can I surrender my reactions to God the Son instead of guarding myself with walls?

_____

_____

What new rhythm would nurture gentleness and gratitude within my heart?

_____

_____

3 | Your Faith in Action

Apply the Devotional Temple Practice:
Take ten minutes to write down what currently fills your heart—worries, hopes, distractions.
Pray over the list, releasing each concern to the Prince of Peace.

Record:
How did my thoughts or emotions shift after entrusting them to Him?

_____

_____

Next Step:
Begin each morning this week by inviting the Son to be the "gatekeeper" of my heart.

4 | Your Wellness Wisdom

Revisit the Devotional Health Coaching Tip:
Emotional stress and toxic thoughts affect the physical heart through tension, hormones, and blood pressure. Stillness, prayer, and forgiveness literally calm the cardiovascular system. Guarding the soul with the peace of Christ guards the body as well.

5 | Your Prayer and Praise

Comment:
Which phrase from today's Devotional Prayer most spoke peace to my heart?

_____

_____

My Prayer Response: _____

_____

_____

6 | Your Revelation

Journal Question:
What one emotion or thought pattern is God the Son inviting me to surrender to Him for protection and peace?

_____

_____

_____

7 | Your Daily Declaration

Repeat the Devotional Affirmation:
I guard the sacred ground of my heart with the love of Christ. Everything I do flows from it.

Today I will ... keep my heart open to Christ Jesus and closed to anything that steals His peace.

DAY 12 – RENEW YOUR MIND

Scripture

Do not conform to the pattern of this world, but be transformed by
the renewing of your mind.
(Romans 12:2 NIV)

Scripture Focus:

Renewal of the mind begins when I exchange worldly thought patterns for the truth of God the Son, the Living Word.

Theme Summary:

Transformation starts in the mind. As I let Scripture reshape my thinking and bring my thoughts captive to Christ, my emotions and choices begin to align with His will.

1 | Your Word Study

Context:

Paul calls believers to present their bodies as living sacrifices and their minds as instruments of transformation. Renewal requires a shift in focus—away from conformity toward spiritual discernment through closeness with Christ.

Key Word:

Renewing (Greek anakainōsis) — to make new again, to renovate, to restore freshness.

Cross References:

- *Ephesians 4:22–24 (NIV) – You were taught, with regard to your former way of life, to put off your old self, which is being corrupted by its deceitful desires; to be made new in the attitude of your minds; and to put on the new self, created to be like God in true righteousness and holiness.*

- *2 Corinthians 10:5 (NIV) – We demolish arguments and every pretension that sets itself up against the knowledge of God, and we take captive every thought to make it obedient to Christ.*

Discovery Questions:

1. Which thought patterns most often pull me away from peace or confidence in Christ Jesus?

_____

_____

2. How does Scripture reframe those thoughts with truth and hope?

_____

_____

3. What new mindset do I need to "put on" to walk in freedom today?

_____

_____

2 | Your Deeper Reflection

Where am I still conforming to patterns of fear, guilt, or perfectionism?

_____

_____

How can I intentionally fill my mind with what is pure, lovely, and praiseworthy (Philippians 4:8 NIV)?

_____

_____

What difference does it make when I start my day with the Christ Jesus, the Living Word, instead of the world's noise?

_____

_____

3 | Your Faith in Action

Apply the Devotional Temple Practice:
Choose one Bible verse to meditate on throughout the day.
Write it on a card or in your Journal or note it in your phone.

Record:
Each time a negative or anxious thought appears, speak the truth of the Bible verse aloud.

_____

_____

Next Step:
Create a short list of "mind renewal verses" to keep nearby for moments of stress.

4 | Your Wellness Wisdom

Revisit the Devotional Health Coaching Tip:
Neuroscience confirms what Scripture teaches: repeated thoughts build neural pathways. Rehearsing truth replaces anxiety with peace. Mindset renewal is both Biblical obedience and mental health practice—training the brain to align with the mind of Christ.

5 | Your Prayer and Praise

Comment:
What phrase from the Devotional Prayer helped me see mindset renewal as grace, not pressure?

_____

_____

My Prayer Response: _____

_____

_____

6 | Your Revelation

Journal Question:

What one recurring thought is Lord Jesus inviting me to bring captive to Him and replace with His truth today?

_____

_____

_____

7 | Your Daily Declaration

Repeat the Devotional Affirmation:

I renew my mind daily by the truth of the Living Word.

Today I will … put on His Helmet of Salvation (Ephesians 6:10–17) and fill my mind with the Gospel of Christ to renew my thoughts.

 # DAY 13 – LAY IT DOWN

Scripture

Cast your cares on the Lord and He will sustain you; He will never let the righteous be shaken.
(Psalm 55:22 NIV)

Scripture Focus:

God the Son never intended for me to shoulder every burden alone. He upholds me when I trust Him enough to release what weighs me down.

Theme Summary:

Surrender is strength. When I lay my worries at the foot of the Cross, He replaces anxiety with assurance of rest and carries what I cannot.

1 | Your Word Study

Context:

David penned this psalm while enduring betrayal and turmoil. Instead of collapsing under fear, he turned his pain into prayer and released the outcome to God.

Key Word:

Cast (Hebrew shalak) — to throw, hurl, or release from one's grasp; to entrust fully.

Cross References:

• *1 Peter 5:7 (NIV) – Cast all your anxiety on Him because He cares for you.*
• *Matthew 11:28 (NIV) – Come to Me, all you who are weary and burdened, and I will give you rest.*

Discovery Questions:

1. Which specific cares am I still carrying that belong in the Shepherd's hands?

   _____

   _____

2. How does believing that the Son *sustains* me change my response to stress?

_____

_____

3. What does it look like to "throw" my concerns on Christ instead of slowly handing them over?

_____

_____

2 | Your Deeper Reflection

Where do I tend to cling to control?

_____

_____

What fears keep me from trusting God the Son with the unknown?

_____

_____

How might peace grow if I made casting my cares at the foot of the Cross a daily practice instead of a last resort?

_____

_____

3 | Your Faith in Action

Apply the Devotional Temple Practice:
Write each burden that comes to mind on a small piece of paper.
Read Psalm 55:22 aloud and release those papers symbolically into Christ's care — toss them into a wastebasket or tear them up.

Record:
How did my body feel after I let go?

_____

_____

Next Step:
Each morning this week, pray before planning: "Lord, I cast my cares on You first."

4 | Your Wellness Wisdom

Revisit the Devotional Health Coaching Tip:
Anxiety keeps your mind and emotions in fight-or-flight mode. Regular release through prayer and Scripture meditation lowers cortisol, steadies the heart, and renews mental clarity. Letting go is good physiology.

5 | Your Prayer and Praise

Comment:
Which phrase in the Devotional Prayer reminded me that my Savior rose from the dead with all power and that His power alone can sustain me?

_____

_____

My Prayer Response: _____

_____

_____

6 | Your Revelation

Journal Question:

What am I holding today that the Savior is asking me to release so He can carry it?

_____

_____

_____

7 | Your Daily Declaration

Repeat the Devotional Affirmation:

I cast my cares on the Lord. He sustains me with unfailing peace.

Today I will ... cast my cares on the Lord and trust Him to sustain me.

# DAY 14 – OVERCOME YOUR FEAR

Scripture

So do not fear, for I am with you; do not be dismayed, for I am your God. I will strengthen you and help you; I will uphold you with my righteous right hand.
(Isaiah 41:10 NIV)

Scripture Focus:

Fear fades when I remember who walks beside me. The strength of the God the Son steadies my heart with His heart when my own feels weak.

Theme Summary:

Courage is not the absence of fear but confidence in the powerful presence of Christ Jesus. As I face my fears through faith, my soul learns His peace.

1 | Your Word Study

Context:

God spoke these words to Israel during exile, assuring them of His unfailing presence. Fear often grows where faith forgets that He is near.

Key Word:

Uphold (Hebrew tamak) — to grasp, hold firmly, sustain, or support from underneath.

Cross References:

- *Psalm 27:1 (NIV) – The Lord is my light and my salvation—whom shall I fear? The Lord is the stronghold of my life—of whom shall I be afraid?*

- *2 Timothy 1:7 (NIV) – For the Spirit God gave us does not make us timid, but gives us power, love and self-discipline.*

Discovery Questions:

1. What fear has been keeping me from peace or obedience?

   _____

   _____

2. How do the promises in Isaiah 41:10 address that specific fear?

_____

_____

3. What would trusting the "righteous right hand" of God the Son look like in practice today?

_____

_____

2 | Your Deeper Reflection

Where does fear show up most often—in my thoughts, my relationships, or my health?

_____

_____

When have I seen the Son's strength replace fear with courage before?

_____

_____

What truth about His character anchors me when I feel anxious?

_____

_____

3 | Your Faith in Action

Apply the Devotional Temple Practice:
Identify one fear that feels heavy today.
Pray, naming it out loud, and visualize placing it in the Savior's strong hand.

Record:
How did my heart feel as I released that fear?

_____

_____

Next Step:
Replace fearful thoughts this week with the following "power verse:"
"I can do all things through Christ who strengthens me." (Philippians 4:13 NIV)

4 | Your Wellness Wisdom

Revisit the Health Coaching Tip:
Mindfulness, deep breathing, prayer, and Scripture meditation relax the body, calm the emotions and renew the mind. God the Son hard-wired peace into our design when we lean into trusting Him.

5 | Your Prayer and Praise

Comment:
Which part of today's Devotional Prayer reminded me that the presence of the Son is stronger than fear?

_____

_____

My Prayer Response: _____

_____

_____

6 | Your Revelation

Journal Question:

What situations do I need to face with faith instead of fear this week?

_____

_____

_____

7 | Your Daily Declaration

Repeat the Devotional Affirmation:

I will not fear, for Jesus is with me—strengthening and upholding me.

Today I will ... walk in courage, trusting Jesus Christ to strengthen and uphold me.

DAY 15 – CHOOSE PEACE

Scripture

Do not be anxious about anything, but in every situation, by prayer and petition, with thanksgiving, present your requests to God. And the peace of God, which transcends all understanding, will guard your hearts and your minds in Christ Jesus.
(Philippians 4:6–7 NIV)

Scripture Focus:

Peace is not passive—it is the product of prayer and trust. As I release my concerns to God the Son, His peace guards my heart and mind.

Theme Summary:

Peace flows from His presence, not your control. When I surrender my anxiety to God the Son with gratitude, His supernatural calm replaces my inner chaos.

1 | Your Word Study

Context:

Paul wrote these words from prison, teaching believers that peace does not depend on circumstance but on communion with Christ Jesus through prayer and gratitude.

Key Word:

Guard (Greek phroureō) — to protect by military guard; to keep under watch. The peace of Christ stands sentry over the believer's inner life.

Cross References:

- *Isaiah 26:3 (NIV) – You will keep in perfect peace those whose minds are steadfast, because they trust in You.*

- *John 14:27 (NIV) – Peace I leave with you; My peace I give you. I do not give to you as the world gives. Do not let your hearts be troubled and do not be afraid.*

Discovery Questions:

1. What worries do I need to present to the Prince of Peace in prayer today?

_____

_____

2. How does gratitude shift my emotional state before I see answered prayers?

_____

_____

3. What would it feel like to let the peace of Christ "stand guard" over my thoughts?

_____

_____

2 | Your Deeper Reflection

When do I most struggle to release anxiety—before prayer or after?

_____

_____

How can I practice gratitude even in situations I cannot control?

_____

_____

What evidence have I seen that peace can coexist with uncertainty?

_____

_____

3 | Your Faith in Action

Apply the Devotional Temple Practice:
Write a short list of your current worries. Pray over each one, thanking Lord Jesus for hearing you.

Record:
How did your mood feel afterward?

_____

_____

Next Step:
Each time anxious thoughts return, breathe deeply and repeat: "The peace of Christ is guarding my heart and mind."

4 | Your Wellness Wisdom

Revisit the Devotional Health Coaching Tip:
Identify three things you enjoy and create for your personal "peace ritual" to calm your heart and mind such as a walk in nature, lighting a candle, writing in your Journal, a cup of your favorite tea, or worship music. Inner peace is a reset: inner tranquility is a gift from Christ.

5 | Your Prayer and Praise

Comment:
Which part of the Devotional Prayer reminded me that the peace of Christ protects my soul from within?

_____

_____

My Prayer Response: _____

_____

_____

6 | Your Revelation

Journal Question:
What anxious thought do I need to surrender to Christ Jesus today to experience His guarding peace?

_____

_____

_____

7 | Your Daily Declaration

Repeat the Devotional Affirmation:
I guard my heart and mind in the peace of Christ Jesus.

Today I will … release my worries in prayer and let the peace of Christ guard my heart and mind.

DAY 16 – REST IN HIS GRACE

Scripture

He does not treat us as our sins deserve or repay us according to our iniquities. For as high as the heavens are above the earth, so great is His love for those who fear Him; as far as the east is from the west, so far has He removed our transgressions from us.

(Psalm 103:10–12 NIV)

Scripture Focus:

Grace removes my shame, guilt and condemnation completely. Rest begins when I believe that God the Son has already paid the price for my sins.

Theme Summary:

Shame exhausts the soul; grace restores it. I can stop striving because the blood of the Lamb has washed my sins away.

1 | Your Word Study

Context:

David marvels that God's covenant love cancels guilt rather than counting it.

Key Phrase:

"As far as the east is from the west" — infinite separation; never to meet again.

Cross References:

- *Micah 7:19 — You will again have compassion on us; you will tread our sins underfoot and hurl all our iniquities into the depths of the sea.*
- *Hebrews 10:17 — Their sins and lawless acts I will remember no more.*

Discovery Questions:

1. Where do I still live as if guilt, shame and condemnation remain?

_____

_____

2. How would my emotions change if I trusted the grace of God the Son with "no more re-membrance"?

_____

_____

3. What rhythm (breath/prayer) can anchor me in His grace today?

_____

_____

2 | Your Deeper Reflection

Where does self-criticism replace gratitude?

_____

_____

What failures, mistakes and regrets do I need to lay at the foot of the Cross?

_____

_____

What does Christ's compassion say to that inner voice of condemnation?

_____

_____

3 | Your Faith in Action

Apply the Devotional Temple Practice:
Write one regret on a slip of paper. Tear it up while praying Psalm 103:12.

Record:
How does your heart feel after releasing it?

_____

_____

Next Step:
When the memory returns, repeat the verse aloud.

4 | Your Wellness Wisdom

Apply the Devotional Healthy Coaching Tip:
Self-condemnation elevates inner turmoil; self-compassion and grace lowers it. Practicing compassionate self-talk rooted in Scripture calms the heart and mind.

5 | Your Prayer and Praise

Comment:
Which part of the Devotional Prayer reminded me that the heart of Christ heals my broken heart from within?

_____

_____

My Prayer Response: _____

_____

_____

6 | Your Revelation

Journal Question:
What guilt is the Savior inviting me to finally lay down?

_____

_____

_____

7 | Your Daily Declaration

Repeat the Devotional Affirmation:
I rest in the unchanging grace of Christ. His blood has washed away my guilt and shame.

Today I will ... rest in Christ's finished work and refuse to rehearse forgiven sins.

DAY 17 – REFRAME THE STORM

Scripture

Consider it pure joy, my brothers and sisters, whenever you face trials of many kinds, because you know that the testing of your faith produces perseverance. Let perseverance finish its work so that you may be mature and complete, not lacking anything.

(James 1:2–4 NIV)

Scripture Focus:

Trials are seasons in which God the Son is molding me and shaping me to maturity.

Theme Summary:

Joy in God the Son is not denial; it is perspective. When I put on His Shield of Faith (Ephesians 6:10–17) and stay centered in Him in the eye of the storm, I can persevere and am strengthened in the storms.

1 | Your Word Study

Context:

James writes to scattered early Christians facing severe persecution and economic hardship. He instructs them to find joy in the trials because they are meant to strengthen their faith and produce spiritual maturity.

Key Word:

Perseverance (hypomonē) — steadfast endurance that remains under.

Cross References:

- *Romans 5:3–4 — Not only so, but we also glory in our sufferings, because we know that suffering produces perseverance; perseverance, character; and character, hope.*

- *1 Peter 1:6–7 — In all this you greatly rejoice, though now for a little while you may have had to suffer grief in all kinds of trials. These have come so that the proven genuineness of your faith—of greater worth than gold, which perishes even though refined by fire—may result in praise, glory and honor when Jesus Christ is revealed.*

Discovery Questions:

1. What is this trial producing in me?

_____

_____

2. Where am I resisting the process?

_____

_____

3. How can I "let perseverance finish its work" this week?

_____

_____

2 | Your Deeper Reflection

How might God the Son be forming patience, humility, or courage through this hardship?

_____

_____

What fear-based story have I been telling myself about this storm, and how might the Son be inviting me to see it differently?

_____

_____

How could shifting my focus from the size of the storm to the presence of Jesus Christ strengthen my emotional resilience?

_____

_____

3 | Your Faith in Action

Apply the Devotional Temple Practice:
Name one current storm.
Write a "growth reframe": *"Through this, Christ is building _____."*

Record:
 Any shift in emotion.

_____

_____

Next Step:
Revisit your "growth reframe" daily.

4 | Your Wellness Wisdom

Revisit the Devotional Health Coaching Tip:
Interpreting stress as "challenge, not threat" reduces cortisol and improves resilience—matching James' invitation to reframe your storm.

5 | Your Prayer and Praise

Comment:
Which part of the Devotional Prayer reminded me that Christ calms the storms in my heart?

_____

_____

My Prayer Response: _____

_____

_____

6 | Your Revelation

Journal Question:
What fruit do I sense God the Son cultivating in this season?

_____

_____

_____

7 | Your Daily Declaration

Repeat the Devotional Affirmation:
I have deep roots of faith in Christ. My resilience is strengthened by every storm.

Today I will ... cooperate with perseverance and look for joy in the growth.

 # DAY 18 – HEAL YOUR BROKEN HEART

Scripture
He heals the brokenhearted and binds up their wounds.
(Psalm 147:3 NIV)

Scripture Focus:
When I am grieving the loss of a loved one or deeply wounded emotionally by life-changing circumstances, God the Son does not hurry my healing. He personally binds my wounds.

Theme Summary:
Grief is holy ground. Inviting Christ Jesus into the heartache begins renewal. By His wounds, I am healed.

1 | Your Word Study

Context:
Post-exile psalm of worship and praise celebrating how despite experiencing trauma and anguish over exile and loss, the Lord had gathered His people again in Jerusalem and that they could trust Him to bring about their restoration and healing.

Key Word:
Binds — to bandage, wrap, and hold together while healing occurs.

Cross References:
- *Isaiah 61:1 — …He has sent me to bind up the brokenhearted, to proclaim freedom for the captives and release from darkness for the prisoners…*
- *Matthew 5:4 — Blessed are those who mourn, for they will be comforted.*

Discovery Questions:

1. What pain needs the loving touch of God the Son today?

   _____

   _____

2. What would "boundaried rest" look like as I heal?

_____

_____

3. Who could safely support me in this process?

_____

_____

2 | Your Deeper Reflection

Where have I hidden my hurt from Christ Jesus?

_____

_____

What would it look like to let Him into those places of my heart that I have been protecting or avoiding?

_____

_____

What happens when I bring my pain to Him in prayer?

_____

_____

3 | Your Faith in Action

Apply the Devotional Temple Practice:
Write a letter to Lord Jesus about the loss or disappointment. End with one sentence of hope.

Record:
Any easing of pain or grief.

_____

_____

Next Step:
Return to this letter later in the week and add any new emotions He brings to the surface.

4 | Your Wellness Wisdom

Revisit the Devotional Healthy Coaching Tip:
Tears release stress chemicals; sleep and gentle movement aid recovery. Hydrate after crying to restore balance.

5 | Your Prayer and Praise

Comment:
Which part of the Devotional Prayer reminded me that Christ heals my brokenness and restores my soul?

_____

_____

My Prayer Response: _____

_____

_____

6 | Your Revelation

Journal Question:
Which wound is Christ Jesus inviting me to uncover so He can bind it?

_____

_____

_____

7 | Your Daily Declaration

Repeat the Devotional Affirmation:
Jesus heals my broken heart and restores joy to my soul.

Today I will ... welcome Jesus into my pain and receive His careful healing.

🕯 DAY 19 – CULTIVATE JOY

Scripture
Do not grieve, for the joy of the Lord is your strength.
(Nehemiah 8:10 NIV)

Scripture Focus:
God the Son is the source of enduring joy and He strengthens me.

Theme Summary:
The joy that God the Son supplies to our soul is a gift, not a mood. Gratitude and worship open the channel.

1 | Your Word Study

Context:
After their return from exile and the completion of the rebuilding of the walls of Jerusalem, Ezra read the Book of Moses. After hearing the Law, Israel wept because they recognized their sins. Nehemiah told the people to stop grieving and redirected them to celebrate God's grace. Joy is found in God's presence.

Key Phrase:
Joy of the Lord — gladness sourced in God's presence and favor.

Cross References:

- *Psalm 16:11 — You made known to me the path of life; you will fill me with joy in your presence, with eternal pleasures at your right hand.*
- *Habakkuk 3:17–19 — Though the fig tree does not bud and there are no grapes on the vines, though the olive crop fails and the fields produce no food, though there are no sheep in the pen and no cattle in the stalls, yet I will rejoice in the Lord, I will be joyful in God my Savior. The Sovereign God is my strength; he makes my feet like the feet of a deer, he enables me to tread on the heights.*

Discovery Questions:

1. Where can I practice gratitude today?

_____

_____

2. What small celebration could honor God's goodness?

_____

_____

3. How has joy given me strength before?

_____

_____

2 | Your Deeper Reflection

When do I equate joy with ease?

_____

_____

How can I receive joy *amid* process?

_____

_____

What small daily practice—gratitude, prayer, or savoring simple joys—helps my heart stay anchored in Christ's joy rather than my circumstance?

_____

_____

3 | Your Faith in Action

Apply the Devotional Temple Practice:
List five blessings (large or small). Read them aloud as praise.

Record:
How your mood shifts.

_____

_____

Next Step:
Choose one joy-building practice to repeat daily for the next 7 days as a soul-strengthening habit.

4 | Your Wellness Wisdom

Revisit the Healthy Coaching Tip:
Gratitude practices improve mental and emotional resilience—embodying "joy is strength."

5 | Your Prayer and Praise

Comment:
Which part of the Devotional Prayer helped me feel covered by Christ's "oil of gladness" regardless of life's circumstances?

_____

_____

My Prayer Response: _____

_____

_____

6 | Your Revelation

Journal Question:
What daily rhythm helps me notice and nurture joy?

_____

_____

7 | Your Daily Declaration

Repeat the Devotional Affirmation:
I am grateful for the goodness of Christ, and the joy of the Lord is my strength.

Today I will ... draw strength from the joy of the Lord and practice gratitude and thanksgiving.

DAY 20 – WALK IN FREEDOM

Scripture
So if the Son sets you free, you will be free indeed.
(John 8:36 NIV)

Scripture Focus:
Freedom is a gift from Jesus, not an achievement. I learn to live what He already secured.

Theme Summary:
Freedom grows as truth replaces lies and grace replaces shame.

1 | Your Word Study

Context:
Jesus confronts bondage to false beliefs: only the Son liberates.

Key Word:
Free indeed — truly, unquestionably free.

Cross References:

- *Romans 8:1–2 — Therefore, there is now no condemnation for those who are in Christ Jesus, because through Christ Jesus the law of the Spirit who gives life has set you free from the law of sin and death.*
- *Galatians 5:1 — It is for freedom that Christ has set us free. Stand firm, then, and do not let yourselves be burdened again by a yoke of slavery.*

Discovery Questions:

1. Which lie still limits me?

_____

_____

2. What truth from the Living Word counters it?

_____

_____

3. What daily choice will help me *stand firm*?

_____

_____

2 | Your Deeper Reflection

What old labels still define me?

_____

_____

What new identity is the Son speaking into my soul?

_____

_____

What thought, habit, or emotional pattern is Christ Jesus inviting me to release to Him so that I can walk more fully in His freedom?

_____

_____

3 | Your Faith in Action

Apply the Devotional Temple Practice:
Write a one-sentence "Freedom Declaration"
(e.g., *In Christ, I am free from _____; I choose _____.*).
Read it morning and evening.

Record:
What emotion, thought pattern, or old habit shifted as I declared my freedom in Christ? What did I notice in my body, my mood, or my mindset as I practiced walking in liberty?

_____

_____

Next Step:
Identify one daily habit that reinforces your freedom in Christ—such as speaking Scripture aloud, beginning the day with gratitude, or releasing anxious thoughts immediately through prayer—and practice it consistently this week.

4 | Your Wellness Wisdom

Revisit the Healthy Coaching Tip:
Living from grace reduces chronic stress and supports steadier energy, clearer focus, and healthier choices. Living from grace restores the mind, will and emotions.

5 | Your Prayer and Praise

Comment:
How did the Devotional Prayer speak to my heart today?

_____

_____

My Prayer Response: _____

_____

6 | Your Revelation

Journal Question:
What step of obedience expresses my freedom in Christ today?

_____

_____

_____

7 | Your Daily Declaration

Repeat the Devotional Affirmation:
I walk in peace, confidence, and joy. The Son has set me free.

Today I will ... live as one Jesus has set free—walking in truth, grace, and peace.

 # My Temple Reflection – Renew Your Soul

A Time of Healing, Renewal, and Peace

Do not conform to the pattern of this world, but be transformed by the renewing of your mind.
(Romans 12:2 NIV)

Leaving the Inner Court

You have completed the second ten days of your Triune Temple Journey™—renewing your soul in the presence of **God the Son**.

This has been a time of emotional release, mental clarity, and mindset renewal.

In this sacred pause, reflect on how Christ Jesus has brought healing, peace, and freedom to the hidden places of your soul.

The *Inner Court* of your Triune Human Temple™ is where inner transformation begins within—and where surrender becomes strength.

My Soul Work – Reflection Prompts

1. My Healing

What emotions or thought patterns has Jesus helped me release or reframe during these ten days?

_____

_____

Where have I experienced His comfort, forgiveness, or peace?

_____

_____

2. My Renewal

How has my mind been renewed through Scripture and prayer?

_____

_____

What truth from God's Word has become my anchor in this season?

_____

_____

3. My Gratitude

What new joys or signs of hope have emerged as I have invited Jesus to renew my soul?

_____

_____

How is He teaching me to extend that same grace to others?

(Use the space below or use the Rebuild Your Temple, God's Way® Journal to write your reflections.)

_____

_____

My Prayer of Renewal

Lord Jesus,
Thank You for renewing my soul and restoring peace to my heart.
Where fear once lived, You have planted faith.
Where sorrow lingered, You have poured in Your joy.
Help me continue to guard my heart and renew my mind with Your Word.
May Your love flow through me as healing to others.
In Your name, I pray, Amen.

My Gratitude Offering

List three ways Jesus has renewed your mind and emotions:

(Use this space or use the Rebuild Your Temple, God's Way® Journal to record a short note of thanks or a favorite verse that strengthened you during this Part II.)

1. _____

2. _____

3. _____

My Extended Reflection

Capture your renewed thoughts and emotions in your Rebuild Your Temple, God's Way® Journal. Write freely about the peace, healing, and clarity Jesus has brought to your soul during this phase of your Triune Temple Journey™.

My Transition to the *Holiest of Holies*

*As I leave the **Inner Court** of renewal,*
*I enter the **Holiest of Holies**—where the Holy Spirit aligns my heart and spirit with*
the heartbeat of my triune God.

PART III – REALIGN YOUR SPIRIT

A 10-Day Journey with God the Holy Spirit —
Living in Communion, Alignment and Purpose

REALIGN

Welcome to the Holiest of Holies

You now stand at the threshold of the *Holiest of Holies*—the sacred dwelling place of **God the Holy Spirit** within your Triune Human Temple™.

Here, worship flows from stillness, and guidance is born of surrender.

This is the space where you no longer strive to find His presence—you simply *abide* in it.

In these next ten days in Part III, you will learn to listen, to trust His whispers, and to walk in harmony with His will.

The Holy Spirit brings alignment, direction, and empowerment so that your entire life—body, soul, and spirit—reflects the glory of the triune God.

As you enter this final stage of the Triune Temple Journey™, release the need to control or understand every step.

Let the Holy Spirit lead you, teach you, and transform you from within.

Your Focus in This Section

- **Commune with the Holy Spirit** — listen for His voice and follow His prompting.
- **Realign your spirit** with His truth and timing.
- **Practice surrender** as worship and obedience.
- **Walk in purpose** as the Holy Spirit empowers you to reflect His glory.

Prayer of Invitation

Holy Spirit,
I welcome You into the *Holiest of Holies* within my spirit.
Quiet my mind and steady my breath so I can hear Your voice.
Align my spirit with Yours, that every thought and action would flow from Your peace.
Where I have resisted Your leading, forgive me and draw me close again.
Breathe new life into my worship, new purpose into my days, and new courage into my obedience.
As I walk through these next ten days, teach me to stay in step with You—resting, listening, and responding in love.
Fill me with Your presence until my life reflects Your glory.
In Jesus' name, I pray, Amen.

Day Overview Table

Day	Title	Scripture (NIV)
21	Dwell in His Presence	Psalm 34:18
22	Abide in the Vine	John 15:4–5
23	Walk By the Spirit	Galatians 5:25
24	Align with His Word	Psalm 119:105
25	Listen for His Voice	John 10:27
26	Worship in Sprit and Truth	John 4:23–24
27	Pray Without Ceasing	1 Thessalonians 5:16–18
28	Surrender Your Will	Luke 22:42
29	Live in Purpose	Ephesians 2:10
30	Reflect His Glory	2 Corinthians 3:18

💛 DAY 21 – DWELL IN HIS PRESENCE

Scripture

The Lord is close to the brokenhearted and saves those who are crushed in spirit.
(Psalm 34:18 NIV)

Scripture Focus:

God the Holy Spirit is not distant from pain. He draws near to comfort, heal, and realign my spirit to Him when my spirit is crushed.

Theme Summary:

Dwelling in the presence of God the Holy Spirit begins with awareness of His nearness, especially in suffering. The Spirit meets my spirit not in perfection, but in surrender.

1 | Your Word Study

Context:

David wrote this psalm while fleeing danger and facing rejection. Even in distress, he discovered the sustaining presence of God. Pain became the place where intimacy with the Lord was renewed.

Key Word:

Close (Hebrew qarob) — near, intimate, in close fellowship or relationship; implies both physical and emotional nearness.

Cross References:

- *Isaiah 57:15 (NIV) – For this is what the high and exalted One says—He who lives forever, whose name is holy: "I live in a high and holy place, but also with the one who is contrite and lowly in spirit, to revive the spirit of the lowly and to revive the heart of the contrite."*

- *John 14:16–17 (NIV) – And I will ask the Father, and He will give you another Advocate to help you and be with you forever—the Spirit of truth. The world cannot accept Him, because it neither sees Him nor knows Him. But you know Him, for He lives with you and will be in you.*

Discovery Questions:

1. How have I experienced the closeness of the Holy Spirit in moments of spiritual weariness?

2. What might I learn about His character through my seasons of weakness?

_____

_____

3. How does the Holy Spirit comfort me when I bring Him my pain rather than hide it?

_____

_____

2 | Your Deeper Reflection

When have I felt too weary to pray yet sensed the Holy Spirit's quiet nearness?

_____

_____

How can I shift from asking "Why?" to asking "Please fill me, Holy Spirit"?

_____

_____

What does it mean for His presence to become my refuge instead of my last resort?

_____

_____

3 | Your Faith in Action

Apply the Devotional Temple Practice:
Set aside time to rest quietly in the presence of the Holy Spirit today.
Bring one area of weariness before Him without words—simply *be still* and receive His comfort.

Record:
What emotions or sensations arose as I sat with Him?

_____

_____

Next Step:
Continue this daily pause with the Holy Spirit this week, allowing His peace to dwell deeply within.

4 | Your Wellness Wisdom

Revisit the Devotional Health Coaching Tip:
Spiritual weariness often manifests physically through fatigue or depression. Stillness and gentle breathing realign the spirit. As I rest in God's presence, my body mirrors His peace—heart rate slows, breath deepens, healing begins.

5 | Your Prayer and Praise

Comment:
Which phrase from the Devotional Prayer reminded me that the Holy Spirit is my Comforter and heals and realigns my spirit with Him?

_____

_____

My Prayer Response: _____

_____

_____

6 | Your Revelation

Journal Question:
Where is the Holy Spirit asking me to acknowledge the weariness, bring it to Him and simply dwell in His healing presence?

_____

_____

_____

7 | Your Daily Declaration

Repeat the Devotional Affirmation:
I am sustained by the Holy Spirit in me, even in my brokenness. He is as close as the breath I breathe.

Today I will … rest in the nearness of God the Holy Spirit, trusting Him to comfort and heal my spirit.

DAY 22 – ABIDE IN THE VINE

Scripture
Remain in me, as I also remain in you. No branch can bear fruit by itself; it must remain in the vine.
(John 15:4–5 NIV)

Scripture Focus:
God the Holy Spirit flows within me. Abiding is not an act of willpower but a posture of surrender that allows the Holy Spirit to produce fruit in and through me.

Theme Summary:
The Holy Spirit keeps me connected to the Vine. As I remain in fellowship with Him, spiritual fruit grows naturally from communion—not from striving.

1 | Your Word Study

Context:
Jesus prepared His disciples for His departure, promising that the Holy Spirit would sustain their union with Him. "Abide" expresses continual dependence on divine life, not self-effort.

Key Word:
Remain (Greek menō) — to stay, dwell, persist, to continue in vital union.

Cross References:

- *Galatians 5:22–23 (NIV) – But the fruit of the Spirit is love, joy, peace, forbearance, kindness, goodness, faithfulness, gentleness and self-control.*

- *1 John 2:27 (NIV) – As for you, the anointing you received from Him remains in you, and you do not need anyone to teach you. But as His anointing teaches you about all things and as that anointing is real, not counterfeit—just as it has taught you, remain in Him.*

Discovery Questions:

1. How do I know when I am abiding rather than striving?

_____

_____

2. Which fruit of the Spirit is most evident—and which needs nurturing?

_____

_____

3. How can I consciously invite the Holy Spirit to flow through my spirit today?

_____

_____

2 | Your Deeper Reflection

When do I lose awareness of the Spirit's indwelling presence?

_____

_____

How does hurry or distraction cut me off from the Vine?

_____

_____

What would change if I moved through the day fully conscious of His presence within me?

_____

_____

3 | Your Faith in Action

Apply the Devotional Temple Practice:
Begin and end your day with this prayer:
"Holy Spirit, keep me abiding in Christ. Let Your fruit flow through me."
Notice how your decisions and emotions align differently when you stay connected.

Record:
What fruit of the Spirit emerged when I paused to abide?

_____

_____

Next Step:
Create a daily reminder (a note, alarm, or symbol) to return your attention to the Spirit's flow.

4 | Your Wellness Wisdom

Revisit the Devotional Health Coaching Tip:
Abiding creates balance. Just as branches depend on steady nourishment, your spirit thrives on rhythm—deep breathing, Scripture meditation, worship music and prayerful pauses. The Holy Spirit teaches us how to remain connected to the Vine.

5 | Your Prayer and Praise

Comment:
Which phrase from the Devotional Prayer helped me experience the Holy Spirit's sustaining presence today?

_____

_____

My Prayer Response: _____

_____

6 | Your Revelation

Journal Question:
What one area of my life needs deeper connection to the Holy Spirit's sustaining power?

_____

_____

_____

7 | Your Daily Declaration

Repeat the Devotional Affirmation:
I remain connected to Christ, and His Spirit renews my strength.

Today I will ... remain in the Holy Spirit's flow, allowing His presence to nourish and produce lasting fruit in me.

♥ DAY 23 – WALK BY THE SPIRIT

Scripture
Since we live by the Spirit, let us keep in step with the Spirit.
(Galatians 5:25 NIV)

Scripture Focus:
The Holy Spirit is my very life; my call is to match His pace—moment by moment, step by step.

Theme Summary:
To "keep in step" means responsive alignment—listening, yielding, and adjusting to the Spirit's leading throughout the day.

1 | Your Word Study

Context:
After describing the fruit of the Spirit, Paul urges believers to let their conduct match their new life. The Spirit is not an accessory; He is the source and rhythm of our walk.

Key Word:
Keep in step (Greek stoicheō) — to walk in line, to follow a prescribed order; to march in sync with a leader.

Cross References:

- *Romans 8:14 (NIV) – For those who are led by the Spirit of God are the children of God.*
- *Galatians 5:16–17 (NIV) – So I say, walk by the Spirit, and you will not gratify the desires of the flesh… They are in conflict with each other, so that you are not to do whatever you want.*

Discovery Questions:

1. Where do I sense the Spirit inviting me to slow down—or to move?

   _____

   _____

2. What habits help me notice His promptings in real time?

_____

_____

3. Which reactions (hurried, defensive, self-led) most often pull me out of step?

_____

_____

2 | Your Deeper Reflection

When have I felt the inner nudge to pause, speak gently, or choose peace—and missed it?

_____

_____

What does the Spirit's pace feel like in my body (unrushed, steady, clear)?

_____

_____

How could I build more margin so I can respond instead of reacting?

_____

_____

3 | Your Faith in Action

Apply the Devotional Temple Practice:
Today, practice "step-checks" before transitions (calls, emails, meals, errands).
Pray: *"Holy Spirit, what is the next right step?"*

Record:
Notable moments when His guidance changed your tone, words, or timing.

_____

_____

Next Step:
Choose one daily anchor (morning prayer, commute, walk) to consciously sync your pace with the Spirit.

4 | Your Wellness Wisdom

Revisit the Health Coaching Tip:
Hurry fuels stress; alignment fosters calm. Pair brief breath prayers with transitions to regulate the nervous system. A slower, Spirit-led pace reduces tension and improves clarity and presence.

5 | Your Prayer and Praise

Comment:
Which line from the Devotional Prayer helped me trust the Spirit's leadership today?

_____

_____

My Prayer Response: _____

_____

_____

6 | Your Revelation

Journal Question:
In what specific situation is the Holy Spirit inviting me to "keep in step" by changing my pace or response?

_____

_____

_____

7 | Your Daily Declaration

Repeat the Devotional Affirmation:
I walk in rhythm with the Spirit, guided by His peace and purpose.

Today I will … keep in step with the Holy Spirit—matching His pace, listening for His promptings, and aligning my actions with His leading.

# DAY 24 – ALIGN WITH HIS WORD

Scripture
Your word is a lamp for my feet, a light on my path.
(Psalm 119:105 NIV)

Scripture Focus:
God the Holy Spirit uses His Word to light my way. As I walk with Him, Scripture becomes revelation—direction for every step.

Theme Summary:
The Spirit and the Word always agree. Alignment begins when I listen to His voice through stillness and Scripture and let His guidance give me direction.

1 | Your Word Study

Context:
Psalm 119 celebrates the Word as the believer's guide and safeguard. The Spirit who inspired Scripture also interprets and applies it within me.

Key Word:
Lamp (Hebrew ner) — a small flame or light that guides one step at a time; *light (Hebrew or)* — illumination, revelation, clarity.

Cross References:

- *John 16:13 (NIV) – But when He, the Spirit of truth, comes, He will guide you into all the truth. He will not speak on His own; He will speak only what He hears, and He will tell you what is yet to come.*

- *2 Timothy 3:16–17 (NIV) – All Scripture is God-breathed and is useful for teaching, rebuking, correcting and training in righteousness, so that the servant of God may be thoroughly equipped for every good work.*

Discovery Questions:

1. How does the Holy Spirit use Scripture to guide me in everyday decisions?

2. What areas of my life need the clarity of His Word right now?

_____

_____

3. How can I invite the Spirit to illuminate, not just inform, my understanding of the Bible?

_____

_____

2 | Your Deeper Reflection

Do I treat Scripture as information or conversation?

_____

_____

When have I sensed a verse come alive through the Spirit's whisper?

_____

_____

What practices help me slow down and listen as I read?

_____

_____

3 | Your Faith in Action

Apply the Devotional Temple Practice:
Before reading Scripture today, pray: *"Holy Spirit, open my eyes to see what You are saying."*
Read one passage slowly; pause after each verse to reflect.

Record:
What phrase or insight felt illuminated?

_____

_____

Next Step:
Commit to daily reading guided by the Spirit, even if for only a few verses.

4 | Your Wellness Wisdom

Revisit the Devotional Health Coaching Tip:
Meditating on Scripture calms and aligns spirit to Spirit. Just as light regulates physical rhythms, the Word regulates spiritual rhythms—reducing fear of uncertainty and restoring connection to the Spirit when internal and external noise grows loud.

5 | Your Prayer and Praise

Comment:
Which phrase in the Devotional Prayer helped me feel the Holy Spirit illuminating God's Word today?

_____

_____

My Prayer Response: _____

_____

_____

6 | Your Revelation

Journal Question:
What specific truth in the Word is the Holy Spirit speaking to me to apply today?

_____

_____

_____

7 | Your Daily Declaration

Repeat the Devotional Affirmation:
I am filled with the Holy Spirit who shines in me, lights my path, and aligns my spirit with His truth.

Today I will ... walk in the light of the Word, allowing the Holy Spirit to guide every step I take.

💗 DAY 25 – LISTEN FOR HIS VOICE

Scripture

My sheep listen to my voice; I know them, and they follow me.
(John 10:27 NIV)

Scripture Focus:

God the Holy Spirit teaches me to recognize the voice of my Lord and Savior. Listening requires quieting distractions and trusting the One who speaks within.

Theme Summary:

The voice of the Holy Spirit is gentle but steady. Alignment deepens as I learn to discern His whisper above the noise of chaos and confusion.

1 | Your Word Study

Context:

Christ Jesus described Himself as the Good Shepherd who calls each sheep by name. Under the new covenant, the Holy Spirit becomes the inner voice that guides, corrects, and comforts.

Key Word:

Listen (Greek akouō) — to hear with understanding, to attend, to obey what is heard.

Cross References:

- *Revelation 3:20 (NIV) – Here I am! I stand at the door and knock. If anyone hears My voice and opens the door, I will come in and eat with that person, and they with Me.*

- *Isaiah 30:21 (NIV) – Whether you turn to the right or to the left, your ears will hear a voice behind you, saying, "This is the way; walk in it."*

Discovery Questions:

1. How do I personally recognize the difference between the Spirit's voice and my own thoughts?

_____

_____

2. What environments make it easier—or harder—to hear Him clearly?

_____

_____

3. How can I cultivate stillness so that obedience becomes my first response?

_____

_____

2 | Your Deeper Reflection

When was the last time I sensed a nudge, conviction, or comfort from the Holy Spirit?

_____

_____

Did I follow it, or question it?

_____

_____

How can I grow in trust by remembering His past faithfulness?

_____

_____

3 | Your Faith in Action

Apply the Devotional Temple Practice:
Today, practice "listening pauses."
When faced with a choice, stop and whisper: *"Holy Spirit, what are You saying?"*

Record:
Any words, impressions, or Scriptures that arise.

_____

_____

Next Step:
Review your notes later to discern patterns of His leading over time.

4 | Your Wellness Wisdom

Revisit the Health Coaching Tip:
Constant noise heightens stress and dulls awareness. Intentional quiet lowers heart rate and enhances focus. Listening to the Spirit teaches the mind and body to rest in divine rhythm instead of reaction.

5 | Your Prayer and Praise

Comment:
Which part of the Devotional Prayer reminded me that the Holy Spirit speaks with love and clarity?

_____

_____

My Prayer Response: _____

_____

_____

6 | Your Revelation

Journal Question:
What decision or situation am I bringing before the Spirit to hear His direction clearly?

_____

_____

_____

7 | Your Daily Declaration

Repeat the Devotional Affirmation:
I quiet and open my spirit. I hear the Holy Spirit's voice with peace and clarity.

Today I will ... listen for the Holy Spirit's voice and follow where He leads with trust and peace.

🤲 DAY 26 – WORSHIP IN SPIRIT AND TRUTH

Scripture

Yet a time is coming and has now come when the true worshipers will worship the Father in the Spirit and in truth, for they are the kind of worshipers the Father seeks.

(John 4:23–24 NIV)

Scripture Focus:

God the Holy Spirit leads me into authentic worship. True worship flows from surrender—spirit to Spirit, heart to heart.

Theme Summary:

Worship is not limited to songs or places. It is a continual response to the Holy Spirit's presence within me, aligning my spirit with His truth.

1 | Your Word Study

Context:

Jesus spoke to the Samaritan woman, revealing that worship would no longer be confined to temples but would take place in the hearts of believers, through the Holy Spirit.

Key Word:

Worship (Greek proskuneō) — to bow, to kiss toward, to show reverence through intimate adoration.

Cross References:

- *Romans 12:1 (NIV) – Therefore, I urge you, brothers and sisters, in view of God's mercy, to offer your bodies as a living sacrifice, holy and pleasing to God—this is your true and proper worship.*
- *Philippians 3:3 (NIV) – For it is we who are the circumcision, we who serve God by His Spirit, who boast in Christ Jesus, and who put no confidence in the flesh.*

Discovery Questions:

1. How does the Holy Spirit transform my understanding of worship from performance to presence?

_____

_____

2. What does it mean to worship "in truth"—not emotion, but alignment with Scripture and sincerity?

_____

_____

3. How can worship become my posture, not just my practice?

_____

_____

2 | Your Deeper Reflection

When do I feel most aware of the Holy Spirit's presence in worship?

_____

_____

Do I approach worship to receive or to give?

_____

_____

How can I invite the Spirit to teach me to worship even in silence, pain, or waiting?

_____

_____

3 | Your Faith in Action

Apply the Devotional Temple Practice:
Choose one moment today to pause and worship—without music or words.
Simply breathe and whisper: *"Holy Spirit, I adore You."*

Record:
What emotions or awareness surfaced as I worshiped in stillness?

_____

_____

Next Step:
Incorporate spontaneous worship moments throughout the week—letting ordinary activities become sacred expressions of love.

4 | Your Wellness Wisdom

Revisit the Devotional Health Coaching Tip:
Worship restores harmony between body and spirit. Singing, deep breathing, or still adoration lowers blood pressure, releases endorphins, and realigns mood. Worship invites the Spirit's peace to flow through the whole person.

5 | Your Prayer and Praise

Comment:
Which phrase from the Devotional Prayer helped me feel the Holy Spirit drawing me into deeper intimacy through worship?

_____

_____

My Prayer Response: _____

_____

_____

_____

6 | Your Revelation

Journal Question:
How is the Holy Spirit inviting me to worship beyond church walls—through my lifestyle, gratitude, and obedience?

_____

_____

_____

7 | Your Daily Declaration

Devotional Affirmation:
I worship in my spirit and in truth. The presence of the Holy Spirit fills my spirit with peace.

Today I will ... worship in Spirit and in truth, letting the Holy Spirit transform every moment into communion with God.

♥ DAY 27 – PRAY WITHOUT CEASING

Scripture
Rejoice always, pray continually, give thanks in all circumstances; for this is God's will for you in Christ Jesus.
(1 Thessalonians 5:16–18 NIV)

Scripture Focus:
God the Holy Spirit makes prayer a lifestyle, not an event. He keeps my spirit connected to Him in every thought, breath, and moment.

Theme Summary:
Prayer without ceasing is constant communion with the Holy Spirit—an ongoing awareness of His presence and participation in every part of life.

1 | Your Word Study

Context:
Paul encouraged believers facing persecution to remain joyful, prayerful, and thankful. Prayer was not meant as endless words, but as continuous relationship empowered by the Spirit.

Key Word:
Pray (Greek proseuchomai) — to commune, to exchange wishes, to align one's will with God's will through conversation.

Cross References:

- *Romans 8:26–27 (NIV) – In the same way, the Spirit helps us in our weakness. We do not know what we ought to pray for, but the Spirit Himself intercedes for us through wordless groans. And He who searches our hearts knows the mind of the Spirit, because the Spirit intercedes for God's people in accordance with the will of God.*

- *Ephesians 6:18 (NIV) – And pray in the Spirit on all occasions with all kinds of prayers and requests. With this in mind, be alert and always keep on praying for all the Lord's people.*

Discovery Questions:

1. How can I cultivate awareness of the Spirit's presence throughout the day?

_____

2. What distractions or doubts interrupt my ongoing conversation with Him?

_____

_____

3. What might "unceasing prayer" look like in my current season of life?

_____

_____

2 | Your Deeper Reflection

Do I limit prayer to certain times, or do I welcome the Spirit into ordinary moments?

_____

_____

How does gratitude strengthen my connection to the Spirit's presence?

_____

_____

What shift happens when prayer becomes my first response rather than my last resort?

_____

_____

3 | Your Faith in Action

Apply the Devotional Temple Practice:
Choose a simple breath prayer to repeat throughout the day:
"Holy Spirit, guide me." or *"Thank You, Holy Spirit."*
Each repetition re-centers your awareness on connection with the Holy Spirit.

Record:
How did this practice influence your mood, focus, or decisions?

_____

_____

Next Step:
Continue your chosen prayer daily for one week, noticing greater peace and sensitivity to the Spirit.

4 | Your Wellness Wisdom

Revisit the Devotional Health Coaching Tip:
Continuous prayer in the Spirit calms the body's stress response. Regular gratitude, mindful breathing and Scripture meditation ease the soul. When prayer becomes rhythm, body, soul and spirit stay balanced.

5 | Your Prayer and Praise

Comment:
Which phrase in the Devotional Prayer reminded me that the Holy Spirit keeps me connected to the Father's heart all day long?

_____

_____

My Prayer Response: _____

_____

_____

6 | Your Revelation

Journal Question:
How can I remain in prayerful awareness of the Holy Spirit during ordinary routines—working, resting, or relating to others?

_____

_____

7 | Your Daily Declaration

Repeat the Devotional Affirmation:
I walk in constant conversation with the Holy Spirit. Prayer is the rhythm of my spirit.

Today I will ... stay in continual communion with the Holy Spirit, letting every breath become a prayer.

# DAY 28 – SURRENDER YOUR WILL

Scripture
Father, if You are willing, take this cup from Me; yet not My will, but Yours be done.
(Luke 22:42 NIV)

Scripture Focus:
God the Holy Spirit strengthens me to say "yes" when surrender feels hard. Yielding my will opens the way for peace, power, and purpose.

Theme Summary:
Surrender is not weakness—it is worship. As I yield to the Holy Spirit's leading, I find freedom from self and alignment with God's heart.

1 | Your Word Study

Context:
In Gethsemane, Jesus Christ faced the agony of obedience. Through the Spirit, He chose submission over resistance, modeling perfect surrender. The Spirit now empowers believers to follow that example.

Key Word:
Will (Greek thelēma) — desire, purpose, intention; God's will is His loving design for the believer's good and His glory.

Cross References:

- *Philippians 2:13 (NIV) – For it is God who works in you to will and to act in order to fulfill His good purpose.*
- *Romans 8:26–27 (NIV) – In the same way, the Spirit helps us in our weakness… the Spirit Himself intercedes for us in accordance with the will of God.*

Discovery Questions:

1. What part of my will resists direction from the Holy Spirit?

2. How does the Holy Spirit help me to trust that His way is better?

_____

_____

3. What peace follows when I stop striving for control?

_____

_____

2 | Your Deeper Reflection

Where in my life am I still "holding on" instead of "letting go"?

_____

_____

How do fear and pride disguise themselves as "good intentions"?

_____

_____

When have I felt the Spirit's gentle prompting to release my plan for His?

_____

_____

3 | Your Faith in Action

Apply the Devotional Temple Practice:
Pray this prayer of release:
"Holy Spirit, help me to yield. Not my will, but Yours be done."
Write down one area you have been trying to control—work, relationships, health—and lay it before Him in prayer.

Record:
How does surrender lighten the physical, emotional, mental or spiritual weight I have been carrying?

_____

_____

Next Step:
Each morning this week, recommit: *"Your will, not mine."*

4 | Your Wellness Wisdom

Revisit the Devotional Health Coaching Tip:
Control creates chronic tension in body and soul; surrender restores calm. Letting go of expectations and outcomes lowers anxiety, supports heart and immune health and promotes serenity. The Spirit's presence teaches the body and soul to exhale—to trust instead of grasp.

5 | Your Prayer and Praise

Comment:
Which phrase in the Devotional Prayer reminded me that surrender is an act of trust and love?

_____

_____

126

My Prayer Response: _____

_____

_____

6 | Your Revelation

Journal Question:

What expectation, outcome or desire is the Holy Spirit inviting me to release fully to Him today?

_____

_____

_____

7 | Your Daily Declaration

Repeat the Devotional Affirmation:

I surrender my will to His will; the Holy Spirit guides my path.

Today I will ... surrender my will to the Holy Spirit's leading, trusting that His plan is perfect and His grace is sufficient.

💛 DAY 29 – LIVE IN PURPOSE

Scripture

For we are God's handiwork, created in Christ Jesus to do good works, which God prepared in advance for us to do.

(Ephesians 2:10 NIV)

Scripture Focus:

God the Holy Spirit activates the purpose He placed within me. I am His masterpiece—designed, equipped, and empowered to fulfill His divine plan.

Theme Summary:

Living in purpose is walking in partnership with the Holy Spirit. My calling is not self-made but Spirit-led—an expression of His creativity through my life.

1 | Your Word Study

Context:

Paul reminds believers that salvation is not earned by works but results in a life of Spirit-led service. The same Spirit who saves also empowers us to accomplish what God prepared beforehand.

Key Word:

Handiwork (Greek poiēma) — masterpiece, something carefully made; the root of our word "poem."

Cross References:

- *Philippians 1:6 (NIV) – Being confident of this, that He who began a good work in you will carry it on to completion until the day of Christ Jesus.*
- *1 Corinthians 12:4–7 (NIV) – There are different kinds of gifts, but the same Spirit distributes them. There are different kinds of service, but the same Lord. There are different kinds of working, but in all of them and in everyone it is the same God at work.*

Discovery Questions:

1. How does knowing I am His masterpiece change how I view my purpose?

_____

_____

2. What "good works" has the Holy Spirit been prompting me to pursue?

_____

_____

3. How can I align my daily actions with the assignments He has already prepared for me?

_____

_____

2 | Your Deeper Reflection

When have I confused busyness with purpose?

_____

_____

What brings me deep joy and peace when I do it? Could that be part of my divine design?

_____

_____

How does the Holy Spirit confirm or redirect my steps toward what truly matters?

_____

_____

3 | Your Faith in Action

Apply the Devotional Temple Practice:
Ask the Holy Spirit to reveal one specific way to serve today—through kindness, encouragement, or prayer.

Record:
How did obedience to that prompting make me feel aligned with His purpose?

_____

_____

Next Step:
Journal three ways I can use my gifts more intentionally for God's glory this month.

4 | Your Wellness Wisdom

Revisit the Health Coaching Tip:
Purpose gives the body energy and the soul endurance. Studies show that people who live with clear purpose experience lower stress and greater vitality. Spiritually, walking in purpose sustains joy and direction.

5 | Your Prayer and Praise

Comment:
Which phrase in the Devotional Prayer reminded me that the Holy Spirit empowers me to fulfill God's purpose?

_____

_____

My Prayer Response: _____

_____

_____

6 | Your Revelation

Journal Question:
What calling or assignment has the Holy Spirit been confirming in this season?

_____

_____

_____

7 | Your Daily Declaration

Repeat the Devotional Affirmation:
I walk in divine purpose; my life is God's masterpiece in motion.

Today I will ... walk boldly in the purpose the Holy Spirit designed for me, using my gifts to glorify God.

 # DAY 30 – REFLECT HIS GLORY

Scripture

And we all, who with unveiled faces contemplate the Lord's glory, are being transformed into His image with ever-increasing glory, which comes from the Lord, who is the Spirit.

(2 Corinthians 3:18 NIV)

Scripture Focus:

God the Holy Spirit transforms me into the likeness of Christ. His glory shines through my surrendered life as I reflect His nature to the world.

Theme Summary:

Transformation is not self-improvement—it is Spirit work. As I bask in His presence, I become a mirror of His glory.

1 | Your Word Study

Context:

Paul contrasts the fading glory of the old covenant with the radiant glory of the new. Through the indwelling Spirit, believers reflect the presence of the triune God from within, not from external law or effort.

Key Word:

Transformed (Greek metamorphoō) — to change form, to be renewed from the inside out; the same word used for Jesus' transfiguration.

Cross References:

- *Romans 8:29 (NIV) – For those God foreknew He also predestined to be conformed to the image of His Son, that He might be the firstborn among many brothers and sisters.*
- *John 16:14 (NIV) – He will glorify Me because it is from Me that He will receive what He will make known to you.*

Discovery Questions:

1. What does reflecting the Spirit's glory look like in everyday life?

2. How has the Holy Spirit changed my attitudes, words, or relationships over time?

_____

_____

3. What areas still need His transforming light?

_____

_____

2 | Your Deeper Reflection

Where have I seen glimpses of the Spirit's transformation in my journey?

_____

_____

When do I most sense His glory shining through my life?

_____

_____

How can I stay humble, remembering that all glory belongs to Him?_____

_____

_____

3 | Your Faith in Action

Apply the Devotional Temple Practice:
Spend a few moments before a mirror today.
Pray: *"Holy Spirit, let Your glory shine through me."*
Reflect on how His presence radiates from within, regardless of outward appearance.

Record:
What fruit or change reflects His work in me this season?

_____

_____

Next Step:
Ask the Spirit to reveal one new way to bring His light to others.

4 | Your Wellness Wisdom

Revisit the Devotional Health Coaching Tip:
Inner transformation manifests outwardly. Peaceful thoughts and gratitude soften expression, improve posture, and even support immune and cardiovascular health. God designed wholeness to shine through every part of us—body, soul, and spirit.

5 | Your Prayer and Praise

Comment:
Which part of the Devotional Prayer reminded me that transformation is the Spirit's work, not mine?

_____

_____

My Prayer Response: _____

_____

_____

6 | Your Revelation

Journal Question:
How is the Holy Spirit inviting me to reflect His glory in my words, habits, and relationships this week?

_____

_____

_____

7 | Your Daily Declaration

Devotional Affirmation:
The Spirit of the Lord lives in me; His glory radiates through my rebuilt temple—body, soul, and spirit.

Today I will ... reflect the glory of the Holy Spirit within me, shining His light wherever I go.

🧡 My Temple Reflection – Realign Your Spirit

A Time of Communion, Alignment, and Rededication

And we all, who with unveiled faces contemplate the Lord's glory, are being transformed into His image with ever-increasing glory, which comes from the Lord, who is the Spirit.
(2 Corinthians 3:18 NIV)

Dwelling in the Holiest of Holies

You have completed this 30-day Triune Temple Journey™—body restored, soul renewed, and spirit realigned.

Now pause in this sacred moment. Breathe deeply. Feel the presence of the Holy Spirit who has been guiding you all along.

This is the *Holiest of Holies* within your Triune Human Temple™—the meeting place between heaven and your heart.

Here, worship becomes stillness. Words fade, and awareness expands.

This is where transformation settles into communion, and communion flows into purpose.

My Spirit Work – Reflection Prompts

1. My Alignment

Where have I sensed the Holy Spirit leading or correcting me these past ten days?

_____

_____

What new rhythm or practice keeps me "in step with the Spirit"?

_____

_____

2. My Restoration and Renewal

How have God the Father and God the Son prepared me to walk more closely with the Holy Spirit?

_____

_____

Which burdens or distractions must I continue to release so that peace remains?

_____

_____

3. My Communion

Describe a moment when you clearly felt God's nearness during this 30-day Triune Temple Journey™.

_____

_____

What truth or phrase will remind you to return to this sacred place each day?

(Use the space below or use the Rebuild Your Temple, God's Way® Journal to write your reflections.)

_____

_____

My Praise and Thanksgiving

Take a few quiet minutes to thank the Holy Spirit for His presence, patience, and power.

List three ways you have experienced His work in your life:

(Use this space or use the Rebuild Your Temple, God's Way® Journal to record a prayer of thanksgiving or a verse that reflects your realignment in the Spirit.)

1. _____

2. _____

3. _____

My Prayer of Thanksgiving

Holy Spirit,
Thank You for leading me into the *Holiest of Holies*.
You have aligned my thoughts with truth and my steps with purpose.
Teach me to remain in continual communion with You—
listening, trusting, and obeying with joy.
Let Your glory shine through my rebuilt temple—
body, soul, and spirit—so that others may see Your light.
In Jesus' name, I pray, Amen.

My Purpose Activation

For we are God's handiwork, created in Christ Jesus to do good works.
(Ephesians 2:10 NIV)

Reflect:

- What specific calling or act of service has God impressed on my heart?

- How will I use my restored strength and renewed faith to serve others?

- Write one sentence beginning with *"The Spirit is calling me to…"*

(Use the space below or use the Rebuild Your Temple, God's Way® Journal to write your reflections.)

_____

_____

_____

_____

_____

_____

My Temple Rededication

Today I rededicate my temple—body, soul, and spirit—to the glory of God.

My Declaration of Rededication:

Lord, this temple is Yours.
Strengthen my body to serve, renew my mind to discern, and ignite my spirit to worship. I choose to walk in alignment with the Father, the Son, and the Holy Spirit—all my days.

Signature: _____   Date: _____

My Transition Statement

Having entered the Holiest of Holies, I now step outward—
carrying His glory into the world through every act of love and obedience.

My Closing Prayer

A Prayer of Dedication and Communion

May God Himself, the God of peace, sanctify you through and through.
May your whole spirit, soul and body be kept blameless at the coming of our Lord Jesus Christ.
(1 Thessalonians 5:23 NIV)

Heavenly Father,
Thank You for walking with me through these thirty sacred days—
for restoring strength to my body, renewing peace in my soul,
and realigning my spirit with Your perfect will.

You are the Creator who formed this temple,
the Redeemer who healed its broken places,
and the Holy Spirit who now fills it with life and purpose.

Father, I dedicate my **body** to You—
that every movement, breath, and act of care would honor Your presence.

Lord Jesus, I surrender my **soul** to You—
that my thoughts, emotions, and desires would reflect Your love and truth.

Holy Spirit, I yield my **spirit** to You—
that I may live each day attuned to Your voice, obedient to Your prompting,
and confident in Your peace.

May my life be a living offering—
a visible expression of Your grace and glory.
Use my restored body, renewed mind, and realigned spirit
to serve, to love, and to reveal Your Kingdom here on earth.

I rededicate this temple—
every heartbeat, every thought, every breath—
to the glory of God the Father,
in the name of Jesus Christ the Son,
and by the power of the Holy Spirit who dwells within me.
Amen.

My Temple Testimony

A Personal Reflection of Restoration, Renewal, and Realignment

Then I heard a loud voice from the throne saying,
Look! God's dwelling place is now among the people, and He will dwell with them.
(Revelation 21:3 NIV)

Your temple has been rebuilt—body, soul, and spirit—through the loving hands of God the Father, God the Son, and God the Holy Spirit.

This is your moment to pause and reflect on the Triune Temple Journey™ you have just completed: the progress, the healing, the surrender, and the new beginnings that now dwell within you.

Your ***Temple Testimony*** is your offering of gratitude—a living altar of praise to the One who restores, renews, and realigns all things.

My Reflection Prompts

1. My Body — Restored by God the Father

What physical habits or rhythms have I reclaimed or begun?

_____

_____

How have I learned to see my body as sacred rather than striving for perfection?

_____

_____

Where do I still feel the Father inviting me to deeper stewardship?

_____

_____

2. My Soul — Renewed by God the Son

How has Jesus healed my emotions, thoughts, or self-image?

_____

_____

What fears or burdens have I laid down at His feet?

_____

_____

Where have I experienced new peace, forgiveness, or joy?

_____

_____

3. My Spirit — Realigned by God the Holy Spirit

How has the Holy Spirit guided or comforted me during this journey?

_____

_____

What new sense of purpose or calling has been revealed?

_____

_____

How am I learning to remain in daily communion with Him?

_____

_____

My Gratitude Offering

List three ways God has revealed His presence through this 30-day Triune Temple Journey™:

1. _____

2. _____

3. _____

Write a short sentence of thanksgiving:

Lord, I thank You for _____ .

(Use this space or use the Rebuild Your Temple, God's Way® Journal to record a short note of thanks or a favorite verse that strengthened you during this section.)

My Closing Testimony Statement

This is my Temple Testimony:

I once _____

But now _____

God has rebuilt my Triune Human Temple™ from the outside in and the inside out.
I dedicate all that I am to His glory.

My Extended Reflection

Continue your reflection in your Rebuild Your Temple, God's Way® Journal.
Use it to record your ongoing testimony of faith, health, and transformation as you walk with God each day.

My Transition to My Temple Covenant

As I complete this testimony of transformation,
I prepare to covenant with God—committing to walk daily in health, holiness, and wholeness,
Rebuilding My Temple, God's Way®.

My Temple Covenant

A Personal Commitment to Rebuild My Temple, God's Way®

*Do you not know that your bodies are temples of the Holy Spirit,
who is in you, whom you have received from God?
You are not your own; you were bought at a price.
Therefore honor God with your bodies.*
(1 Corinthians 6:19–20 NIV)

Today, I stand before my triune God—
grateful for His mercy, transformed by His grace, and empowered by His Spirit.

Over this 30-Day Triune Temple Journey™, He has restored my body, renewed my soul, and re-aligned my spirit.

Now I joyfully enter into covenant with Him, committing to honor His dwelling place within me.

My Covenant Promises

1. I will honor God with my body.

I commit to treat my body as His sacred temple—nourishing it, resting it, and strengthening it for His glory.

2. I will renew my mind with His truth.

I will choose thoughts, words, and emotions that align with the love and peace of Christ Jesus.

3. I will walk in the Spirit.

I will listen for the Holy Spirit's leading, obey His promptings, and live each day in alignment with His will.

4. I will live as a testimony of grace.

I will use my restored health and renewed faith to serve others, encourage hearts, and reflect the light of God's Kingdom.

My Prayer of Dedication

Heavenly Father,
I dedicate this Triune Human Temple™ to You.
May my life continually reflect Your goodness and glory.
Keep me faithful to the habits of holiness and the rhythms of grace You have taught me.
When I am weary, restore me. When I am distracted, realign me.
When I am tempted to give up, remind me that You dwell within me.
I covenant today to walk with You daily, rebuilding and maintaining this temple, God's way.
In the name of the Father, the Son, and the Holy Spirit, I pray, Amen.

My Signature of Covenant

Signed: _____

Date: _____

Witness (optional): _____

My Declaration of Covenant

My temple belongs to God.
I am His dwelling place—restored, renewed, and realigned for His purpose.

My Extended Reflection

Use your Rebuild Your Temple, God's Way® Journal to write a personal reflection or prayer of thanksgiving for this covenant moment.

Record how you plan to live out this commitment through daily habits of faith, health, and obedience.

My Faith and Health Habit Tracker

Living Out My Temple Covenant—One Faithful Step at a Time

Let us not become weary in doing good, for at the proper time
we will reap a harvest if we do not give up.
(Galatians 6:9 NIV)

Your Triune Human Temple™ has been restored, renewed, and realigned.

Now, this tracker helps you maintain the rhythm of worship through simple, consistent habits—faithful actions that honor God through daily stewardship of body, soul, and spirit.

Remember: this is not about striving for perfection but walking in partnership with the Holy Spirit.

Each small, faithful step is an act of worship.

How to Use This Tracker

1. Choose a 30-day or 90-day period to continue your Triune Temple Journey™.

2. Select one or two habits per area—body, soul, and spirit—that reflect your personal covenant.

3. Mark your progress daily with a check, a heart, or a reflection word (*grace, strength, peace*).

4. At the end of each week, record a short praise for how you've seen God's faithfulness.

My Faith and Health Commitments

Temple Area	My Chosen Habits	Why It Matters to My Walk with God
Body (Restore)	e.g., Hydrate daily; Stretch 10 minutes; Prepare nourishing meals; Sleep 7 hours	My body is His dwelling place.
Soul (Renew)	e.g., Gratitude journaling; Replace negative thought; Sabbath rest; Forgive quickly	Jesus renews my mind and heals my emotions.
Spirit (Realign)	e.g., Morning prayer; Daily Scripture reading; Worship walk; Listen for the Spirit's voice	The Holy Spirit guides and empowers my purpose.

(Use this chart to plan and personalize your next 30–90 days of faith and health goals.)

My Weekly Tracker

For the week of _____

Week	Body	Soul	Spirit	Praise Report / Reflection
Week 1	☐ ☐ ☐ ☐ ☐ ☐ ☐	☐ ☐ ☐ ☐ ☐ ☐ ☐	☐ ☐ ☐ ☐ ☐ ☐ ☐	
Week 2	☐ ☐ ☐ ☐ ☐ ☐ ☐	☐ ☐ ☐ ☐ ☐ ☐ ☐	☐ ☐ ☐ ☐ ☐ ☐ ☐	
Week 3	☐ ☐ ☐ ☐ ☐ ☐ ☐	☐ ☐ ☐ ☐ ☐ ☐ ☐	☐ ☐ ☐ ☐ ☐ ☐ ☐	
Week 4	☐ ☐ ☐ ☐ ☐ ☐ ☐	☐ ☐ ☐ ☐ ☐ ☐ ☐	☐ ☐ ☐ ☐ ☐ ☐ ☐	

(You may copy or print this page for continued use.)

My Weekly Reflection Prompts

At the end of each week, take a few minutes to reflect:

- What progress am I celebrating this week?

- What obstacle did I overcome by faith?

- Where did I sense God's strength or peace?

- What habit do I need to release or adjust for next week?

(Write your reflections in this Bible Study Workbook or in your Rebuild Your Temple, God's Way® Journal.)

My Monthly Praise Summary

When you complete your 30 or 90 days, pause and reflect on God's faithfulness:

- How has God strengthened your body, renewed your soul, and realigned your spirit?

- What new fruit of the Spirit (Galatians 5:22–23) do you see blossoming in your life?

Write a short prayer of thanksgiving:

Father, thank You for _____.

(Write your praise reports in this Bible Study Workbook or in your Rebuild Your Temple, God's Way® Journal.)

My Encouragement to Continue

Progress, not perfection, honors God.

Every act of obedience, no matter how small, **Rebuilds Your Temple, God's Way**® *from the outside in and the inside out.*

Continue Your Triune Temple Journey™

Congratulations!

You have completed this *Rebuild Your Temple, God's Way® Faith and Health Bible Study Workbook: A Companion Bible Study Guide to the 30-Day Faith and Health Devotional*—a Triune Temple Journey™ from the *Outer Court* to the *Inner Court* to the *Holiest of Holies* of your Triune Human Temple™.

But you have just begun the transformation process—a journey of holistic healing that continues day by day.

You have rebuilt the *Outer Court* of your temple by restoring your body, renewed the *Inner Court* of your temple by healing your soul, and entered the *Holiest of Holies* by realigning your spirit with God the Father and God the Son through God the Holy Spirit.

Your Triune Human Temple™ is being restored to health and wholeness—not through perfection, but through His continual presence and grace.

Remember: Healing is not a destination; it is a divine rhythm of abiding, trusting, and growing in His grace.

Continue your Triune Temple Journey™ of faith and health by:

- Abiding in God's presence through worship, Scripture meditation, prayer, and community.

- Practicing the daily rhythms of the new habits you have begun to form—nourishment, movement, rest; surrender, gratitude, peace; communion, harmony, and purpose.

- Serving God and others with your renewed strength—let your story inspire others, stir up their faith and reignite their hope.

Please accept the invitation to let **Rebuild Your Temple, God's Way®** continue with you on your Triune Temple Journey™ to guide and support you.

Visit **www.rebuildyourtemplegodsway.com** to explore transformational Christian health coaching programs and resources designed to help you reclaim and maintain a life of health and wholeness—body, soul, and spirit—God's way.

Restore Your Body. Renew Your Soul. Realign Your Spirit.™

www.ingramcontent.com/pod-product-compliance
Lightning Source LLC
Chambersburg PA
CBHW041615120626

46551CB00003B/458

* 9 7 9 8 9 9 3 8 1 2 9 8 4 *